W9-AYO-917

marks noted 9/5/96

THE
EGYPTIAN
WORLD

TB

Published in 1989 by Warwick Press,
387 Park Avenue South, New York, N.Y.10016.
First published in 1989 by Kingfisher Books Ltd.
Copyright © Kingfisher Books Ltd. 1989.

6 5 4 3 2 1

Printed in Italy

Library of Congress Catalog Card No. 89-50002
ISBN 0-531-19068-4

The publishers wish to thank the following for
supplying photographs for this book:

9 ZEFA; 12 Peter Clayton; 14 Margaret Oliphant;
15 Illustrated London News Picture Library; 16
Petrie Museum; 17 Egypt Exploration Society; 19
top ZEFA, *bottom* UNESCO; 21 British Museum;
22 Flinders Petrie Museum; 24 Peter Clayton; 26
Max Hirmer; 27 Werner Forman Archive, Egyptian Museum, Cairo; 28, 30 Peter Clayton; 33
Ancient Art and Architecture Collection; 34
ZEFA; 36, 37 *top* Michael Holford; 37 *bottom*
British Museum; 39 Peter Clayton; 42 Michael
Holford; 43 Photoresources; 44 Ancient Art and
Architecture Collection; 45 Egyptian Museum,
Cairo; 47 Oriental Institute, Chicago; 48 Michael
Holford; 49 *top* Ancient Art and Architecture
Collection, *bottom* Scala; 50 British Museum; 51
top Peter Clayton, *bottom* Lucy Cooper; 52
British Museum; 54, 57 Michael Holford; 61
British Museum; 63 *left* British Museum, *right*
Peter Clayton; 66 British Museum; 68 Manchester
Museum; 70 Peter Clayton; 71 NHPA; 74 Peter
Clayton; 76 Ancient Art and Architecture Collection; 77 Photoresources; 82 ZEFA; 83 Griffith
Institute, Oxford; 84 Peter Clayton; 85 *top*
Granard Rowland Communications, *bottom* Institute of Archaeology, London; 86 *right* Sonia
Halliday Photographs, *left*, 87 *top* Peter Clayton,
bottom Lucy Cooper.

The publishers also wish to thank the following
artists for contributing to the book:

Nick Cannan: pp. 20–1, 29, 38, 70, 71, 88;
Vanessa Card pp. 40–1, 58, 67 (bottom); Stephen
Conlin pp. 10–11, 17, 32, 35, 39, 46, 51, 53, 62,
67 (top), 69, 76, 78–9; Kevin Maddison pp. 13
(left), 23, 25, 27, 31, 55, 59, 60, 64–5, 73, 80–1;
Malcolm Porter pp. 11, 13 (right), 45, 47, 82;
David Salariya p. 75, cover.

THE EGYPTIAN WORLD

Margaret Oliphant

Warwick Press
New York/London/Toronto/Sydney

932
OLI

CONTENTS

THE EGYPTIAN WORLD   10

THE LAND OF EGYPT   12

THE EVIDENCE   14
Rediscovery of Egypt   14
Modern Archaeology   16
Writing and Decipherment   20

BEFORE THE PHARAOHS   22

THE OLD AND MIDDLE KINGDOMS   24

KING AND COURT   26
Kingship   26
Government and Administration   28

RELIGION   30
Priests and Ritual   30
Gods   32
Temples   34

THE NEW KINGDOM   36
History   36
War and the Army   38
Neighbors   40
The Amarna Age   42

IMPERIAL DECLINE   44

FOREIGN KINGS   46

GREEKS AND ROMANS   48

EVERYDAY LIFE   50
An Egyptian Village   50
A Nobleman's House   52
Eating and Drinking   54
Hunting and Fishing   56
Music and Games   58
Clothing and Jewelry   60
Crafts and Industry   62
Farming   66
Medicine and Doctors   68
The Scribes and Literature   70
Education   72

THE LAND OF THE DEAD   74
Mummification   74
Funerals and Burial Equipment   76
Pyramids   78
Rock Tombs and Funerary Temples   82
The Boy King   84

EGYPT THEN AND NOW   86

TIMELINE   88
GLOSSARY   89
LOOKING FURTHER   90
BIBLIOGRAPHY   90
INDEX   91

The Egyptian World

When you think of ancient Egypt, you probably have in your mind a picture of pyramids and of mummies in museums. But did you also know that whenever you pick up a pen to write on paper, you are doing something that the Egyptians began to do more than 5000 years ago? Today, we are closer in time to the Romans than the Romans were to those first Egyptians who built the pyramids and invented papyrus for writing on.

For more than a thousand years Egypt was one of the most powerful countries in the Middle East. Later, Egypt was ruled by the Macedonian Greeks and then by the Romans. It subsequently became an important center of Christianity before the arrival of Islam in the 7th century A.D.

Three thousand years of history

In this book we shall look at the ancient Egyptian world, which lasted for over 3,000 years. Of course there were many changes during that time, but there was also much that remained the same. One of the reasons for this was that until quite late in its history, Egypt was isolated from its neighbors. The people lived in the valley of the river Nile, which was protected from the outside world by the desert to the east and west and by the

Above: Colossal statues forming the facade of the temple of Ramesses II, which was moved to a higher position between 1964 and 1968 in order to protect it from the river waters.

Mediterranean to the north. Rather like an island, the valley was cut off from invasion and outside influence, and so a way of life developed that continued for centuries.

Another reason for this continuity was that the Egyptian way of life was well suited to its surroundings. In a country with little or no rain, life centered on the river, which provided water for crops and for people and animals to drink; houses and boats were built from river mud and reeds.

Every scrap of land was needed for fields and houses, so the dead were buried in tombs in the desert and cliffs. As the Egyptians believed in an afterlife, they provided the dead with everything needed to continue the pleasures of life in the next world and they painted their tombs with scenes of daily life. The dry climate has preserved many of these paintings and objects, and from them, as well as from their writings, we can now learn a great deal about the ancient Egyptians.

Below: The pyramids at Giza.
Royal tombs built by the 4th Dynasty kings Khufu, Khephren, and Menkaure.

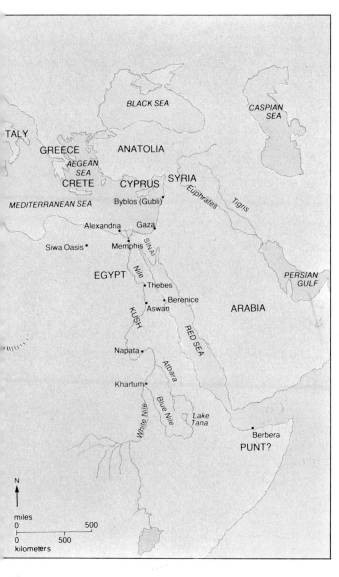

Cleopatra's Needle, Thames Embankment, London. One of a pair of obelisks erected by Tuthmosis III at the Sun Temple at Heliopolis. It was taken to Alexandria during the time of Augustus. In the 14th century it was felled by an earthquake. It 1878 it was transported to England.

Map showing the land of Egypt and the surrounding countries.

Right: Fortress of Buhen in Nubia. A mud-brick fortress built in the Middle Kingdom. Egyptian expansion into Nubia in search of gold ed to the building of forts to hold Egyptian garrisons.

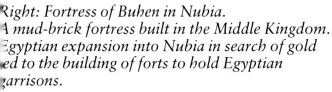

Below: Mortuary temple of Queen Hatshepsut at Deir el-Bahri. Originally the courtyards were full of trees, plants, and statues.

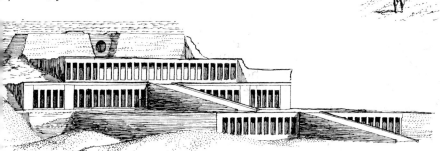

11

The Land of Egypt

The world of the Egyptians centred on their great river, the Nile. To understand Egyptian life, we need to imagine a world of clear blue skies where the sun shines brightly in the intense summer heat and where no rain falls, except for a little near the coast. The river provided the life-giving water which is why Herodotus, a Greek historian, called Egypt "the gift of the Nile".

On the map you will see that green fields lie either side of the river, while beyond is the sandy waste of the desert, which was called *Dashre*, "the Red Land". Here nothing grew and only wild animals and scattered tribesmen (the hated Sand Dwellers) lived. Sometimes Egyptians went into the desert to obtain gold, precious stones, salt, and minerals. They also went there to bury their dead, in tombs away from the land of the living.

Along the river banks the farmers, villagers, and townspeople lived. The river's long journey through Egypt to the Mediterranean Sea begins far away to the south, in Central Africa and Ethiopia. Every year heavy rainfall and melting snow swell the rivers that feed the Nile. Nowadays dams regulate the river's flow, but until recently it began to rise in July and flooded the valley in August and September. This was called the *inundation*. When the water receded, the land was covered in silt which was rich and fertile; the Egyptians called their country *Keme*, "the Black Land."

With careful *irrigation* the Egyptians could grow two crops a year. Sometimes there was a poor flood and when that happened there was a famine, while too much flooding brought destruction. One of the most important things to remember about Egypt is that without the Nile the land would all be desert—nothing could grow there and nobody could live there.

The division of the land

The land could only be cultivated as far as it was possible to bring water. Beyond this point the Black Land gave way to the Red Land. The contrast between the fields is striking. It is even possible to stand with one foot at the edge of the crops and the other in the desert.

Egypt was also divided into two regions, Upper Egypt and Lower Egypt. For 800 miles, from Aswan to the Mediterranean Sea, the Nile flows from south to north, so that, confusingly, the southern region is called Upper Egypt and Lower Egypt is in the north. Once they were two lands, ruled separately; they were united early in Egypt's history but the division survived in the title given to every king: "king of Upper and Lower Egypt."

View of the river Nile, cultivation area, village and burial ground at Beni Hasan. Both the houses and the tombs are built above the cultivation at the desert's edge.

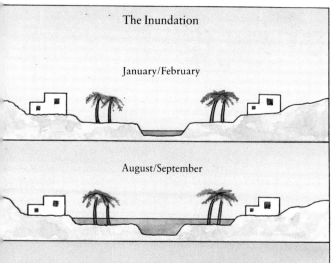

The Inundation

January/February

August/September

From June the water level of the river Nile rose to cover the land in August/September. The river reached its lowest level in January/February.

The Two Lands of Egypt

In Lower Egypt the river splits into channels to reach the sea; this is called the Delta. It was once largely marshland with shallow lakes and lagoons. Gradually, parts were cultivated and the thickets of reed and papyrus were crossed by irrigation channels leading to pastures and vineyards. From delta cities such as Tanis, merchants traded with the Levant (the countries on the east coast of the Mediterranean) which the Egyptians called "the Great Green."

Another fertile area was the oasis of the Faiyum, which was linked to the Nile. Many people lived here. South of the Delta lay Memphis, the ancient capital and an administrative center. The pyramid tombs of the early kings were at the desert's edge nearby. Like most Egyptian cities, Memphis was on the river, the main highway of the country.

In the south, the cliffs edging the desert were closer to the river, so there was less land for growing crops. The most important city was Thebes, a later capital and a great religious center. Across the river was the desolate Valley of the Kings. Gold was mined in the hills of the Eastern Desert.

In Upper Egypt the First Cataract of the Nile at Aswan acted as a natural barrier, forming Egypt's traditional southern boundary. Aswan was a great trading center and many exotic products of Africa passed through there. Beyond this lay the land of Nubia, made up of Kush and Wawat. This area was a major source of gold for the Egyptians.

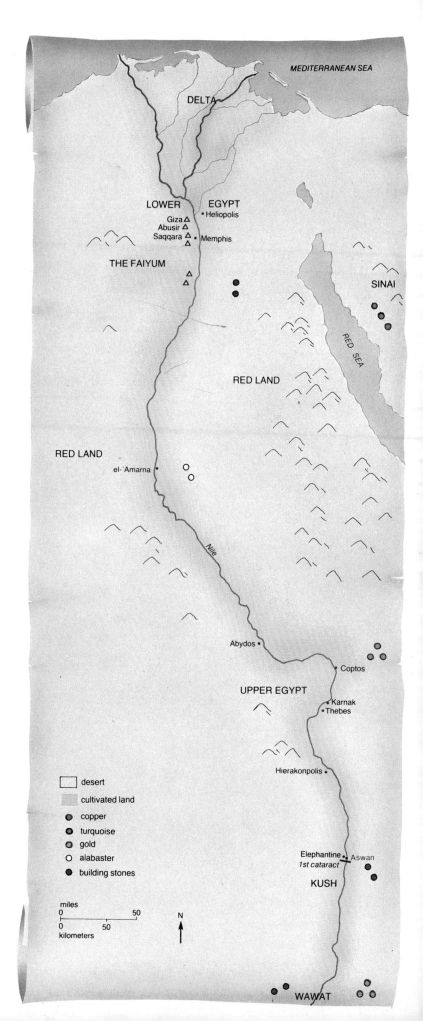

MEDITERRANEAN SEA

DELTA

LOWER EGYPT

Giza △
Abusir △
Saqqara △ • Memphis
• Heliopolis

THE FAIYUM

△
△

SINAI

RED LAND

RED SEA

RED LAND

el-'Amarna •

Nile

Abydos •

Coptos •

UPPER EGYPT

• Karnak
• Thebes

Hierakonpolis •

□ desert

cultivated land

● copper

◐ turquoise

◉ gold

○ alabaster

● building stones

Elephantine • • Aswan
1st cataract

KUSH

miles
0 _____ 50

0 ____ 50
kilometers

N

WAWAT

The Evidence

Rediscovery of Egypt

How is so much known about people who lived thousands of years ago? How do we know what the Egyptians called their country and when they built the pyramids? Well, this information is based on *evidence*.

Some evidence comes from what archaeologists call *material remains*, which may vary from tiny fragments of pottery to remains of huge buildings. There is also *written evidence*, both Egyptian and that of other people who wrote about them. All this information can give us a picture of the Egyptian world. But it is only part of the picture, because we do not have all the evidence.

How evidence was lost

Much evidence has been lost completely and will never be found, while some still awaits discovery. Why have some things been lost and not others? There are several reasons for this.

For example, Egypt's dry climate has preserved the paintings and contents of many tombs. Some tombs, however, were looted either thousands of years ago or more recently. So whether or not a tomb was robbed is as important a factor to its survival as climate.

Some buildings survived because they were built of durable stone and continued to be used and repaired. Some temples were later converted into Christian churches. Others were dismantled and their stones used for new buildings.

Above: Pietro della Valle examining mummies at Dahshur. This Italian traveler visited Egypt in the 16th century and returned to Europe with many antiquities and inscriptions. He later published a report of the inscriptions.

Left: Napoleon encouraged his troops before the Battle of the Pyramids. "Four thousand years of history look down upon you."

THE EVIDENCE

With the spread of Christianity, Egypt's ancient traditions were gradually abandoned and lost. In time, so too was the language (page 20). Such changes meant that although monuments like the pyramids survived and could be seen, nobody knew what they were. It was to be many centuries before the secrets of ancient Egypt were revealed.

The Revival of interest

Interest in the ancient world revived during Europe's Renaissance period and from the end of the 16th century travelers visited Egypt and brought back to Europe mummies and other ancient objects, which are generally called *antiquities*. Most of the evidence has been acquired since the beginning of the 19th century.

When Napoleon invaded Egypt in 1798, 200 scholars accompanied the soldiers. Their duty was to explore and describe the country. Although the French were defeated after only three years, the work of these scholars laid the foundations for the study of Egypt. Through the books that they wrote, other scholars could study copies of ancient monuments and written texts. Among these was the Rosetta Stone (see page 21), which provided the key to the ancient Egyptian language.

The 19th Century

The French expedition had set a fashion for visiting Egypt and through the 19th century many Europeans traveled there. Huge collections of antiquities were gathered for collectors and museums in Europe.

In those early days a lot of evidence was lost in the search for rare and beautiful objects, as tombs were opened with battering rams and even gunpowder. In other cases, local people robbed tombs for antiquities to sell to dealers.

Royal mummies found as a result of tomb robberies being taken from their hiding place at Deir el-Bahri. They were taken by river to Cairo.

Modern Archaeology

Gradually treasure-hunting gave way to proper excavation, and Egypt was one of the first countries to create an antiquities service. Occasionally, however, illegal digging led indirectly to great and exciting discoveries.

In 1871 a family of tomb-robbers found a collection of mummies in a secluded rock shaft in the Valley of the Kings. For ten years they stole things and sold them to dealers in Thebes. When at last their secret was uncovered, 36 royal mummies and some 6,000 objects were found. Even more amazing was the discovery that 3,000 years earlier, these mummies had been removed from their tombs by officials and hidden in this remote spot to prevent further tomb robberies.

How the past is reconstructed

Since the early days of *Egyptology* (the study of ancient Egypt), an enormous amount of evidence has been found. Many museums now have large Egyptian collections and if you have visited one, you will probably have noticed that all the objects carry descriptions of what they are, when they date from and sometimes from where they come. All this information is the result of the work of scholars who have carefully *reconstructed* the history and way of life of the Egyptians.

Some of them are *archaeologists* who visit Egypt regularly to *excavate* or dig and record a chosen site. But that is only part of their work, as time is spent on research before they start excavat-ing and afterwards they must publish what they have found. On a dig there is also a surveyor, someone to copy the inscriptions, and a technical artist to draw the objects.

Other scholars do their work in libraries, museums, and laboratories. There are also specialists in language, history, art, and pottery. The diet of the Egyptians is studied by analyzing food remains, seeds, and animal bones.

Piecing together the evidence

Gradually all the different pieces of information are put together. Sometimes part of an object or document is in one place and the rest is somewhere else. From time to time, a missing piece turns up years later.

Tomb-robbers sometimes tried to have more stolen objects to sell by breaking them or, in the case of papyri, by cutting them up. In 1935 a Belgian scholar was examining antiquities recently given to the Museum in Brussels. Imagine his excitement when he realized that he was looking at the top half of a papyrus that had been in England for nearly a century.

The new papyrus was the missing section of a story that began on yet another papyrus which had been in the British Museum since 1857. It was the account of a trial that took place in Egypt in 1126 B.C. The accused were none other then the family of robbers of the royal tombs in the Valley of the Kings.

Workmen excavating the Temple of Ptah at Memphis in 1910. Flinders Petrie directed excavations at Memphis for six years until the outbreak of World War I in 1918. Memphis was the ancient capital of Egypt and was an administrative center for 3,000 years. The large site (8 × 4 miles) was waterlogged for part of the year and could only be excavated from January, when the inundation subsided, until March or April. A huge labor force was required and pumps were used to remove the subsoil water which lay near the surface. One of the early discoveries was the Temple of Ptah, the god of craftsmen and patron god of the city.

THE EVIDENCE

Sir Flinders Petrie

Sir Flinders Petrie (1853–1942), known as "Father of Pots," was one of the pioneers of modern archaeological method. He excavated at many sites all over Egypt. Although he made some spectacular discoveries, his work was more important in providing a framework of information about the different areas and periods. Petrie was the first to understand the value of small objects and the importance of recording everything found, even though its significance might not be obvious at the time. His life was spent digging, recording, sorting, and bringing order to Egypt's ancient past.

Sequence Dating

One of Petrie's major contributions to archaeology was his invention of the concept of *Sequence Dating*. Working back from the styles of the earliest historical period, he arranged the *prehistoric* pottery of 900 selected tombs into *chronological order*. In arranging the types, he assumed that certain styles did not suddenly appear and disappear, but gradually became more popular and then, equally gradually, less so. Those objects closer to each other in time would have certain similarities of style, while those farthest away from each other would have fewer resemblances.

Seven successive stages can be seen on the chart, each linked to the one before and after by at least one similar shape. Petrie then divided the pottery sequence into equal sections numbered 30 to 80 to allow for future discoveries.

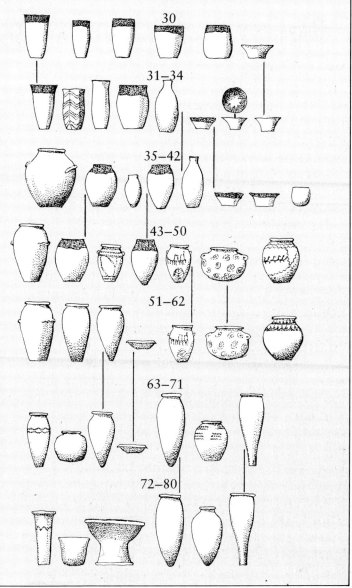

n 1981 The Egypt Exploration Society began work on a Survey of Memphis, with the aim of studying the site from every aspect through its entire history. Already the central ruin field has been mapped and over 150 excavation sites have been located and recorded. The excavation and survey reports, together with the material on the pottery that has been found, have been put on a computer. All the inscriptions are also being recorded. This careful recording by modern Egyptologists continues the tradition of thorough, scientific study introduced by Petrie. This photograph shows the Ptah Temple 75 years after the photograph on the opposite page.

Modern Archaeology

Written Evidence

Of course, it is not often that there is such a close and tidy link between the written and excavated evidence. A lot of what we know comes solely from what the Egyptians wrote. Although the Egyptians did not write history books like the Greeks or Romans, their history can be pieced together from their writings. Kings and nobles wrote about the great events of their lives and there are letters, legal documents, and various other records.

An amazing discovery was made in 1887 when a large collection of clay tablets was found at el-Amarna, which had been the capital of Egypt for a few years in the 14th century B.C. They were written in Akkadian, the language of the Babylonians, which at the time was used for diplomatic purposes, when communicating with foreign peoples. This diplomatic archive contained letters from various Middle Eastern rulers to the Pharaoh and they help us to understand Egypt's relations with its neighbors (page 40).

Excavated Evidence

Much of the excavated evidence comes from tombs preserved by the dry desert climate or from stone-built temples. The Egyptians believed in a life after death, so tombs were filled with everything that would be needed in the next life: clothing, jewels, food, furniture, tools, and games. These objects and the tomb-paintings, which were scenes from daily life, are some of the main sources of evidence for Egyptian life. The most famous and complete tomb to be found was that of Tutankhamun, in the Valley of the Kings (see page 83).

Places where people lived are called *settlement sites*. When these are excavated, we can get a much clearer picture of the way people lived and the homes they lived in. We know quite a lot now, for example, about the town of el-Amarna, where the clay tablets were found, because it has been excavated by a number of different teams. Another such excavation has been at the workers' village of Deir el-Medinah, home of the craftsmen at the royal tombs in the Valley of the Kings. (It was here that the tomb robbers lived.)

Some sites are found by accident, while others such as large temples and the pyramids at Giza have always been visible. Some are found by systematic exploration or survey. The sites are recorded and copies are made of inscriptions so that they are not lost, as it may be many years before there is enough money to excavate the site. Obtaining the evidence is a long and complex business and needs many skilled people.

Rescue Archaeology

Nowadays *rescue archaeology* is important as the pace of modern construction increases. In recent years teams of Egyptologists, archaeologists, and other scholars from many countries, have worked together to record and preserve the archaeological remains of Nubia. The building of a huge dam at Aswan has flooded the Nile Valley to create an enormous lake.

In 1960 an international appeal was launched to save the antiquities in the area about to be flooded. A survey was carried out and everything that was not removed was copied and recorded. Several temples and other monuments were moved to places of safety.

One temple was dragged on a rolling platform to a site several miles from the banks of the lake while another was rebuilt near Aswan. The temple of Philae was dismantled, each piece was individually marked, and then it was completely rebuilt on another island where it is now above the water level.

The two temples of Abu Simbel were cut into huge blocks, some weighing 30 tons, and were remounted at the top of the cliff, backed by enormous dome-shaped structures. As each of the colossal statues is about 100 feet high, the successful completion of this project was an incredible achievement. The resited temples were opened in September 1968 and are now seen by many tourists who visit Egypt.

Top: One of the temples at Abu Simbel in its new position, farther away from the water.
Bottom: Part of the facade of the temple being dismantled and removed from its original site. The operation took place between 1964 and 1968.

Writing and Decipherment

Without the written remains of the Egyptians, nothing would be known of their history. The Egyptians were one of the first peoples to use writing. Their earliest writing dates back to about 3100 B.C. and is called *hieroglyphic* meaning "sacred carved inscription." This is a Greek term; the Egyptians called their writing "the god's word."

Hieroglyphics began as simple picture-writing, where a picture-sign, or *hieroglyph*, conveyed the meaning of an object. A method evolved for representing ideas and actions. Picture-writing was then made even more flexible by the development of signs for *sounds*.

If you were putting spoken English into picture-writing, you could make the word "belief" from the sounds of the words "bee" and "leaf," which could be written as 🐝 🍃.

Let us look at an example of how this worked in Egyptian. First of all, this picture-sign of a mouth meant the object "mouth" and was pronounced "ro" ⏝. There was also a word with the same sound "ro," which meant "toward." In order to show the difference between the two meanings, "toward" was written as the picture-sign, while "mouth" was written as the picture-sign with a little vertical sign beneath it ⏝. Finally, the picture-sign was also used for the sound "r."

So the Egyptians used the same sign in three different ways: as an *idea* or *sense-sign* for "mouth" ⏝; as a *word-sign* for "toward" ⏝ and as a *sound-sign* for "r" — for example in the word for "name," which was *ren* in Egyptian and was written ⏝. On the right you can see an alphabet of hieroglyphic symbols, which are only a few of the many signs an Egyptian schoolboy had to learn before he could become a scribe.

Hieratic and demotic writing
Another form of writing developed from hieroglyphics, called *hieratic*. If you look at the illustration (right), you can see that the signs on the left are like rounded and squiggled versions of the pictures on the right, as if the writer was in a hurry. Whereas hieroglyphic writing was used on buildings and tombs, hieratic and *demotic* (a later and simpler form) were usually written in ink on papyrus. Hieratic was more formal, while demotic was the writing commonly used in everyday life. For a long time all three systems were used.

After Alexander the Great's conquest in 332 B.C. (page 48) the rulers of Egypt were Greek and it was the language of the Greeks that was used in courtly circles. Some inscriptions during this time were written in both Greek and Egyptian, but gradually fewer and fewer people knew how to write Egyptian. Eventually, with the spread of Christianity, all knowledge of the old ways of writing vanished. The last surviving hieroglyphs were written in A.D. 394.

One form of Egyptian survived. It was called *Coptic*. It was the survival of this language that eventually enabled scholars to decipher hieroglyphs.

In 1799 French soldiers digging fortifications in the Delta made a wonderful discovery: they found an inscription which was written by priests in 196 B.C. in hieroglyph and demotic as well as in Greek. It is called the Rosetta Stone and is now in the British Museum.

Champollion, a brilliant young French scholar of ancient languages, used this inscription to decode the hieroglyphic symbols. From his knowledge of Greek and Coptic, he was able to identify the hieroglyphic characters of the name "Ptolemy," which was written in a *cartouche*— the encircled name of the king:

P T O L M Y S

The hieratic writing on the left is an address on a letter sent in 2002 B.C. that never reached its destination. The hieroglyphs on the right are a transcription and show how hieratic developed from more detailed picture signs. The address says: "The overseer of Lower Egypt, Re'nofre." The letter is from Deir el-Bahri.

THE EVIDENCE

The Rosetta Stone

He compared this with a cartouche from another inscription which had some of the same signs and read it as:

KLIOPADRA

Gradually he built up a sign list from other royal names and titles. In 1822 he made known his discoveries. Although there was still a great deal of work to be done, hieroglyphics could at last be read again.

Champollion

SIGN	OBJECT DEPICTED	APPROXIMATE SOUND VALUE
	Egyptian vulture	glottal stop
	flowering reed	*i*
	1. two reed-flowers 2. oblique strokes	*y*
	forearm	a guttural sound not found in English
	quail chick	*w*
	foot	*b*
	stool	*p*
	horned viper	*f*
	owl	*m*
	water	*n*
	mouth	*r*
	reed shelter	*h*
	twisted flax	slightly guttural *h*
	placenta	*ch* (as in Scottish *loch*)
	animal's belly	slightly softer *ch*
	1. door bolt 2. folded cloth	*s*
	pool	*sh*
	hill-slope	*k* sound, rather like *q* in *queen*
	basket with handle	*k*
	stand for jar	hard *g*, as in *gate*
	loaf	*t*
	tethering rope	*tj*
	hand	*d*
	snake	*dj*

Before the Pharaohs

Many stories and plays begin with a prologue which explains the background to what you are going to read about or see. This chapter is the prologue to the story of Ancient Egypt.

We have already seen that the pyramids were 2,000 years old by the time of the Roman Empire. There was an even longer timespan between the arrival of the first people in the Nile Valley and the building of these monuments. For thousands of years people gradually acquired the skills that would eventually enable them to create a highly civilized way of life.

First settlements in the Nile Valley

The last Ice Age ended around 10,000 B.C. The grasslands of North Africa began to turn into the areas that are now the Sahara and the Eastern Desert.

Both animals and people needed water to survive. As the plains and river courses dried up, they moved into the Nile Valley, where the river was fed by melting snow and tropical rains far to the south. Here, the river and its marshy swamps and pools were full of plants, animals and fish.

The people were nomadic hunters, constantly moving from one place to another. In time, they began to settle in one place, waiting to harvest the wild crops that grew in the Valley. Later they learned to grow wheat and barley.

The annual flooding of the Nile laid down fertile soil, making it easy to grow crops, so easy that all that had to be done was to scatter the seed, tread it into the earth and watch it grow. No tilling or fertilizer was needed. The people of the Valley gradually became settled farmers, learning to make use of animals to help them. Dogs and cats were trained to assist with hunting and birds and animals were caught for breeding.

The development of irrigation

As more food was produced, people became healthier and stronger and so lived longer. As the population grew, more and more land had to be cultivated for food. Irrigation methods were developed so that water could reach land that was not flooded during the inundation.

Irrigation required co-operation between large numbers of people. It was probably as a result of this that groups of people began to become more organized. Leaders were needed to negotiate agreements between different groups of people concerning water rights and other similar matters.

Gradually small groups grew into village communities. As more of the Valley was cultivated, the districts grew larger and more villages were set up. Some villages and their leaders grew wealthier and more powerful than others, and the smaller communities of a district began to look to them for protection. In this way, powerful chiefs emerged who controlled each district or *nome*.

During this time, people became more and more skilled. By 5000 B.C. some communities had made sickles out of wood and flint; grain was milled with querns and stones; rush mats were woven to

Wall-painting from the brick-built tomb of an important chief at Hierakonpolis. The man grappling with two lions is not a usual Egyptian subject; the ships also appear to be foreign.

ine the grain storage pits and a coarse kind of linen was made from flax. Jewelry, ivory combs, decorated pottery, and carved stone objects were all in use by 3500 B.C. It was not long before people began to use objects made of copper.

The late prehistoric period

Great changes took place in Egypt in the late prehistoric period. There seems to have been some contact with people from western Asia, which stimulated new developments in Egypt. Mud-brick buildings began to replace those of reeds and matting and, most importantly, the first hieroglyphic writing appeared.

In time, a number of districts grouped together under the leadership of the most powerful chief. In the south of Egypt, Hierakonpolis became the center of power. Archaeological evidence shows that elaborate and wealthy tombs were built here for a few princes.

In the north, power was transferred from one town to another. Finally, after a series of conflicts, the details of which are not fully known, north and south Egypt were united in around 3000 B.C. According to tradition, Menes was the first ruler of the Two Lands. It is possible, but not certain, that Menes and Narmer, who is described below, were one and the same person.

This slate palette commemorates Narmer's victories in Lower Egypt. On the right, Narmer wears the White Crown of Upper Egypt. The text under the falcon reads "the god Horus offers the captive delta to the King." On the left, Narmer wears the Red Crown of Lower Egypt and inspects the battlefield. This is the earliest surviving complete object from Pharaonic Egypt and appears to be the first written record of an historic event

PICTORIAL REPRESENTATION

Victorious king clubs his enemy

IDEA-SIGNS/SOUND-SIGNS

Horus (the king)

papyrus

land/territory

PICTURE HIEROGLYPHS

harpoon

province

catfish (nar)

chisel (mar)

23

The Old and Middle Kingdoms

Egypt's ancient history spans 3,000 years. For convenience, it is divided into several phases, the main three being the Old, Middle, and New Kingdoms. The kings, or *pharaohs* of Egypt are grouped into *dynasties* or families. There are 31 dynasties and Egyptologists often describe a period by its dynasty number.

During the 300 years from the reign of Menes to the first Old Kingdom rulers, the foundation of the future state was laid. As irrigation works were extended, the country grew prosperous and a centralized system of administration was developed.

Expeditions abroad

Egyptians traded with the Levant and with Nubia and visited the mines in Sinai. We know about these expeditions from *inscriptions*. Some from the tombs of high officials are quite detailed.

One of these officials, called Harkhuf, visited Nubia and wrote to the king to tell him that he was bringing back a pygmy. The king wrote back instructing that great care should be taken:

> "... When he lies down at night get twenty worthy men to lie around him in his tent. Inspect ten times at night. My majesty desires to see this pygmy more than the gifts of the mine-land and of Punt ..."

(The mine-land was Sinai and Punt was the region from where incense and other exotic items came).

The rulers of the first two dynasties were buried at Abydos and Saqqara in rectangular flat-topped brick tombs, called *mastabas*. The remains which have been found of the objects put in these tombs show that the kings were wealthy.

Egypt entered a new stage of wealth and greatness under the reign of the kings of the 3rd Dynasty. This period is known as the Old Kingdom and its wealth is reflected in the building of great stone monuments in which the kings were buried. The first of these was the tomb of Djoser, the step pyramid built at Saqqara by the architect and *vizier* Imhotep. In the picture on page 25 you can see Djoser and Imhotep visiting the great pyramid complex.

During the next 400 years, a series of great pyramids was built. The two which were built at Giza for Khufu and his successor, Khephren, were the greatest of all. They are still the most famous monuments of the Egyptian pharaohs.

The rise of the nobles

The important nobles were buried in *mastaba* tombs which were built around the pyramids. Some nobles chose instead to be buried in rock-cut tombs in cliffs of the areas where they had lived and governed.

The nobles became a wealthy group, receiving gifts of land from the king and being exempted from taxes. They became increasingly powerful and independent. At the end of the 6th Dynasty, rival kings appeared and civil war broke out. The government was weak and ineffective and the country was split in two, with one king in the north and another in the south.

This troubled time lasted for about 150 years, until 2040 B.C. It came to an end when Mentuhotep, the ruler of Thebes, brought the whole country under his control. His family ruled from Thebes and were buried there.

Western Asiatics trading eye-paint with Khnumhotep, governor of the Eastern desert in the reign of Sesostris II. Their bright garments and leather boots have been carefully recorded. (Beni Hassan 1895 B.C.).

The 12th Dynasty

The 12th Dynasty kings preferred to rule from the Memphis area. They built their pyramids around the Faiyum, which was drained at this time. The old trading links were re-established and mining expeditions were sent to Sinai again. Nubia became an Egyptian province after several hard campaigns. Fortresses, including Buhen (page 11), were built to control the Nubians.

Under the strong Middle Kingdom kings, the country prospered. Gradually the authority of the king weakened. People from the east, known as the Hyksos, took advantage of this weakness and invaded the north. They allied themselves with the Nubians, who regained their independence. Southern Egypt remained free of Hyksos rule, but had to pay them tribute with gifts. Although the Hyksos adopted the Egyptian way of life and their gods, the Egyptians could never forgive them for their conquest.

King and Court

Kingship

The god-king

The Egyptians believed that their king was a god. He was not only the gods' representative on earth but also the living son of the chief god, Re'. He was believed to have godlike powers.

One of these powers was his command over the Nile. Little rain fell in Egypt, so the timing and level of the flooding of the Nile each year were important to the country's prosperity. Each year the king performed ceremonies which were intended to make the river rise at the required time.

Another ceremony linked to the king's magical powers over the river was called "Opening the Dikes." This was carried out when the floodwaters were falling and the new land was about to emerge. The king cut the first sod of earth with a pick. Later, he sailed in his stage barge through an opening in the dikes to open the new basin. Here the water collected into a pool. Irrigation channels were dug, leading from the basin into the land to be cultivated and the water flowed into them.

These rituals were an important part of kingship because the river and irrigation brought life to Egypt. The king, acting as a god, was therefore seen to have control over life itself.

The heb-sed festival

Another important ritual for the king was a ceremony in which he had to run a fixed course, in order to prove to his people that he was still strong enough to rule the land and control the unseen forces of evil. This was called the *heb-sed* festival and was usually held after the king had reigned for 30 years.

The duties of kingship

The king had several names and titles. The full list consisted of a group of five names, each standing for different aspects of kingship. The basic functions of the king were religious, so pictures on the walls of temples always show the king performing the daily ritual of making offerings to the gods, although in reality priests often did this for him (page 30).

The king was also head of the army, the law, and the government. He had a duty to keep Upper and Lower Egypt united. Although he was absolute king of Egypt, he governed the country with the help of many officials.

Relief in Djoser's Step Pyramid showing the king running on a ceremonial course, part of the heb-sed *festival, when the king's health and vigor were reviewed.*

This is king Khephren, one of the kings of the 4th Dynasty. The royal god Horus in the shape of a falcon is sitting on the throne, lending his protective strength to the king.

The king's regalia

The king was sometimes required to wear ceremonial clothes and to carry certain symbols of his authority, such as the *scepter*, the *crook*, and the *flail*. There were different crowns for special occasions, but most frequently he wore the red and white double crown to emphasize that he was king of the Two Lands of Egypt. He wore the tail of a giraffe or bull attached to the back of his belt. One important part of his regalia was a false beard, held in place by a band around his jaw. In procession he was accompanied by a fan-bearer who carried a fan of ostrich feathers; originally this had been made of woven grass. At his coronation, the king wore all his regalia and a kilt. For the celebration of the *heb-sed* festival, also known as the Jubilee, a long cloak was part of the ceremonial robes.

The king's palace

The king lived in a palace, called *Per'ao*, which meant "the Great House." The name *Pharaoh*, which is used as the title for Egyptian kings, is derived from this word.

Palaces were built to impress. Each new Pharaoh tried to outdo his predecessor by building a lavish new palace. These were usually constructed of brick with painted rooms and they contained every possible comfort.

The Pharaoh's day was highly structured and organized. He was dressed by his attendants every morning after the ceremonial purification and his day was then filled with affairs of state, receptions, ceremonials, and the administration of justice.

From Menes, the ruler who united Upper and Lower Egypt, to Cleopatra, the last Queen, the kingship endured as the symbol of power, stability and order.

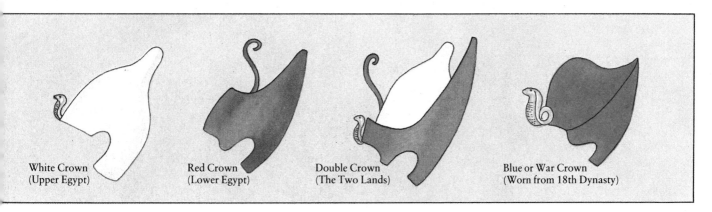

White Crown
(Upper Egypt)

Red Crown
(Lower Egypt)

Double Crown
(The Two Lands)

Blue or War Crown
(Worn from 18th Dynasty)

Government and Administration

The Pharaoh had many officials to help him rule Egypt. Originally these were close relatives and in time these positions were passed down from father to son.

These officials administered a strong and efficient system of government. By the time of the Old Kingdom they made a census every two years of all the fields in the country, for taxation purposes; they also made a census of all cattle.

Taxation provided much of the Pharaoh's wealth. The Pharaoh needed funds for the upkeep of his household, to pay the salaries of the officials and to make gifts to the nobles. He controlled all foreign trade and owned mines and quarries. Funds were also needed to equip military and mining expeditions and to carry out foreign policy. One important duty of the officials was to build up reserve stocks of grain for the years of low flooding, when there were shortages of food.

The officials kept a list of landowners and tenants. Every year officials would visit the farming land and measure people's fields in order to work out how much each farm was likely to produce. One of the factors also taken into account was the probable height of the inundation. This was calculated from measurements of the height of the river shown on *nilometers* at Aswan and elsewhere. Other officials came to calculate the amount of tax each landowner should pay. Later they came to collect it, by force if necessary.

The duties and rights of the people

Everyone was required by law to work for the Pharaoh on irrigation and building projects. Those who were wealthy enough usually paid others to do these duties for them. The *corvée duty*, as it is called, was imposed on people during the time of the inundation, when the fields were flooded and no work could be done on the farms. The Pharaoh owned all the land and everything in it, so he and his officials could demand the use of anyone's animals or pieces of equipment whenever they wished.

Everyone had the right to be heard in any legal dispute but punishments for offences were severe. Sometimes a whole family would be punished for a crime committed by one of its members. Occasionally officials were corrupt and gave unfair judgements and sentences. If people wished, they could then appeal to the Pharaoh. In such a case, they would probably have been heard by the *vizier*, who was the highest official in the land.

The vizier had immense responsibilities and was rather like a prime minister. There were two viziers, one for Upper and the other for Lower Egypt. They were both appointed by the Pharaoh. On the front cover of this book you can see a vizier traveling on a boat on an official inspection tour of the country.

Prince Rahotep and his wife Nofret. Rahotep was a general and high-priest at Heliopolis during the 4th Dynsasty (2723–2563 B.C.). These painted statues are from a tomb at Meidum.

THE NOME-SIGNS OF LOWER EGYPT

Nomes

Nome is a Greek term for the districts or provinces into which Egypt was divided for administrative purposes. In many cases their origins went back to pre-dynastic times when independent communities grew up, centered on a local town or village. With the emergence of Egypt as a unified and centralized state, they lost their independence, but in times of weak central government or anarchy, the country reverted quite naturally to these divisions.

Each nome had its own god and the *nome-signs* were primitive pictures of these gods. The nomes were all named after their symbols, which in early times were carried on a standard.

By the 5th Dynasty the 22 nomes of Upper Egypt were fixed. The 20 signs above are those of Lower Egypt in the Greek and Roman period. They are based on lists from temples of that time.

1. *White wall:* (Memphis) Signs for "wall" and "white."
2. *Thigh:* (Letopolis) An ox-thigh.
3. *Western nome:* Idea-sign for "west."

4. *Southern shield:* The goddess Neith's shield with a reed meaning "south."
5. *Northern shield:* Papyrus plant for "north."
6. *Mountain bull:* For "mountain" and "bull."
7. *Western harpoon:* Boat with harpoon and sign for "west."
8. *Eastern harpoon:* Boat with harpoon and sign for "east."
9. *Anedjti:* Name of the nome god.
10. *Great black bull:* Capital, Athribis.
11. *Heseb bull.*
12. *Cow with calf:* Capital, Sebenytos.
13. *Undamaged scepter* or *Ruler of Anedjti:* (Heliopolis).
14. *Eastern nome:* Sign for "east" with pot-stand meaning "upper."
15. *Ibis:* Capital, Hermopolis.
16. *The Fish:* Capital, Mendes.
17. *Behdet:* The place of the throne.
18. *Upper (Egyptian) royal child:* Capital, Bubastis.
19. *Lower (Egyptian) royal child:* Capital, Tanis. The rear of the animal means "lower."
20. *Sopdu:* The nome god.

Religion

Priests and Ritual

Religion and festivals

Religion played an important part in Egyptian life, providing help for people against their enemies and the hostile forces of nature.

Ordinary people did not normally go to the great temples to worship. Instead, they had small statues of gods in their homes; a favorite was the plump god of dancing and music, the dwarf god Bes. They would also offer up prayers and gifts in small local shrines to a god who had a special meaning for them.

Most people only took part in the religion of the great state gods, such as Amun or Osiris, during the religious festivals. The god's statue was carried in a procession, accompanied by the Pharaoh, priests and nobles. This was called "the coming forth" because the god had come out of his house, the temple. The festivals were splendid holiday occasions, celebrating important events of the year, such as the harvest or the inundation of the Nile. They also took place when one god visited another in a neighboring temple.

The Pharaoh was believed to be the gods' son on earth. It was therefore his duty to feed and protect the gods and to keep everything in order for them. By doing so, it was believed that he preserved the order and harmony of the world. Egyptians called this state of order or balance *Ma'at*, and maintaining it was an important part of their religion. Without Ma'at there would be disorder and chaos.

Naturally the Pharaoh had many other functions to perform, so the daily religious duties of caring for the gods were often carried out by priests on the Pharaoh's behalf.

The morning ritual

Before sunrise there would be great activity in the temple kitchens as meat and bread were prepared for the gods' meals. At dawn, the god was woken by a choir of priests and priestesses, as they processed toward the door leading to the sanctuary, where the shrine containing the statue of the god was kept. Only the priests, who had purified themselves, went into the sanctuary. They removed the statue from its shrine and took off the clothing and make-up fom the previous day. The statue was then cleaned by the burning of sweet-smelling incense. After being newly dressed and adorned, the god was ready to be served with food and drink.

This "breakfast" was later removed and eaten by the priests as part of their payment. At midday and in the evening, further meals were provided and at night the statue was put to bed in the shrine. The final part of the daily ritual was the purification of the room with incense. All footprints were carefully swept away.

Most priests spent only three months of the year in the temples and lived at home with their families for the rest of the year, working as scribes, lawyers or doctors. They were well paid, well educated and highly respected. As time went by, they became a powerful group.

Pharaoh Seti I offers flowers to Horus.

RELIGION

The life of a priest

Although priests were allowed many privileges, they were also expected to lead simple lives and to eat and drink moderately. They were not allowed to eat certain foods, such as pork and fish. To remain pure, they had to bathe twice during the day and twice at night. They were required to shave their heads and bodies every three days. Their clothes were made of fine white linen and they wore white sandals.

There were several grades of priests under the high priest of each god. Some of them wore distinctive clothes to show their position. The Reader Priest, for example, who was responsible for the correct recitation of the ritual, wore a sash across his chest.

In the picture below you can see the priests performing the morning ritual in the sanctuary; one priest carries a flare to provide light, as it was always very dark in the temples.

Gods

The Egyptians worshiped many different gods. At first their gods were the elements and forces that affected their daily life and existence. For example, the sun, the storm, and the wind, or the river that brought a good harvest. Each had to be encouraged and thanked, or dissuaded from doing harm. Fierce animals such as lions and crocodiles were also worshiped as gods, together with useful and friendly animals.

Gradually the Egyptians began to think of the gods as having some human qualities, and so they came to be represented in human shape. Some, however, retained the head of an animal. Each region had its own special god, although in time a few of these became national or *universal* gods, worshiped throughout the land.

Many stories were told about the gods. These are sometimes rather complicated, as the stories tended to change over the years and often varied from place to place.

The origin of the world

There were several stories explaining the origin of the world. According to one, the world was originally a watery chaos from which the sun god *Atum* emerged on a mound. (The sun god was later called *Re'*).

Atum created the gods of air and moisture and their daughter was *Nut*, the sky goddess. She was portrayed as a woman whose body curved to form the arch of heaven. Her brother *Geb*, the earth god, was also her husband and was shown as a man lying on the ground to form the earth.

They had four children, about whom there were many myths. *Osiris* was the god of the Underworld, the dead king. In pictures he is represented as a mummified king. He was also a god of vegetation and he introduced agriculture and wine growing into the country. He was called "the good being" or "the perfect one" and was one of the best-loved of the gods.

Osiris was murdered by his brother *Seth*, lord of the desert and god of storms and violence. Seth cut up the body of Osiris and scattered it throughout Egypt. *Isis*, the wife and sister of Osiris, together with her sister *Nephthys*, found the pieces. Using magic they put him together again.

NUT   GEB

SETH   ISIS   OSIRIS   NEPHTHYS

PTAH   AMUN   HORUS   HATHOR

MA'AT   SEKHMET   HAPI

Isis wore a throne symbol on her head and was of special importance to kings. After Osiris had been brought back to life, Isis conceived their son *Horus* the heavenly falcon god, who was also the living king. Secretly, Isis brought up her son in a remote part of the Delta and when he was old enough he took up the struggle with Seth, to avenge his father. After many contests, Horus defeated Seth.

Horus and Seth

There are several myths about the struggle between Horus and Seth. In one, Seth stole the *udjat*, the magical eye of Horus, who retrieved it after a violent struggle. In another story, a series of contests took place between the two enemies, before a tribunal of the gods. These stories represent the struggle between good and evil forces, but they were also linked to an earthly contest between ancient kings for the crown of Upper and Lower Egypt.

Another god closely associated with the king was *Amun*, the god of Thebes, who ultimately became the supreme state god. He was identified with the sun god, Re', as *Amun-Re'*. Amun's great temple was at Thebes (page 34).

Some gods were associated with the activities of ordinary people. *Ptah*, the local god of Memphis, was the patron of craftsmen and was believed to have invented the arts. Ptah's wife, the lion-headed goddess *Sekhmet* was a war goddess. She brought destruction to the enemies of Re'. Her weapons were arrows and the hot desert winds were believed to be her fiery breath.

The gods of love and prosperity

The goddess of love and of music and dance was *Hathor*, often showed with a *sistrum*, an instrument like a rattle. She was usually shown in human form with a sun disk and cow horns on her head. According to an ancient legend, she had once raised the youthful sun up to heaven on her horns.

Ma'at personified the basic laws of existence, without which there would be disorder. She was the goddess of truth, order, and law. Judges were regarded as her priests. The Egyptians believed that the heart of each person who died was weighed on the scales of justice against the ostrich feather of Ma'at, the symbol of truth, which the goddess wore on her head.

The Nile, as we have seen, brought fertility to the land of Egypt. The god of the Nile in flood was *Hapi*, shown as a long-haired man with papyrus on his head; he carried offering tables laden with produce. He was thought to live in a cave from which the Nile flowed out. The annual flooding of the river was called "the arrival of Hapi."

These are only a few of the most important of the hundreds of gods worshiped by the Egyptians. Even when new gods were introduced, the old ones were not discarded.

Shu, the air-god, separates his daugther Nut, the sky-goddess, from the earth-god Geb. By day the sun-god Re' sailed his boat between heaven and earth, resting at night in the body of Nut, to be born again each morning.

Temples

The temples were the homes of the gods. They were thought to be the places where the Pharaoh, as the god on earth, could communicate with and serve the gods in heaven.

There were different types of temples. Some, called *cult temples*, were dedicated to one particular god, who might be a local god or one of the great state gods. There were also *mortuary temples* linked to the tomb complex of the dead Pharaoh. When Pharaohs were buried in pyramids, these temples stood near the pyramid at the end of a *causeway*, a long avenue that led up from another small temple in the valley near the river. Later, in the Valley of the Kings, they were attached to the tombs. In these temples the statue of the god was represented as the dead Pharaoh.

Sun temples were open to the sky. In place of the god's statue, there was a squat *obelisk* or column, topped with a gold cap shaped like a small pyramid.

Most of the surviving temples in Egypt are cult temples, like the great temple of Amun at Karnak, which was the largest of all the temples ever built.

The temple enclosure
Great care was taken to keep the temple pure and isolated from the ordinary world, so it stood in a sacred enclosure surrounded by a wall. The great sloping walls of the temple itself were called called *pylons*. These were covered with pictures of the gods. Outside the pylons were a pair of tall gold-capped obelisks, covered with hieroglyphs. When there was a festival, tradesmen were allowed to erect booths in front of the pylons.

Behind the pylons was a great open courtyard which led to the *hypostyle hall*. This was designed to resemble a huge papyrus thicket, so that the columns supporting the roof were decorated to look like plants. The floor was painted to look like water, from which the plants appeared to grow. Overhead, the ceiling was painted like the starry heavens.

At the very back of the temple building was the sanctuary. Here, in the darkest part of the temple, was the god's shrine. Near to the temple was the "sacred lake," where the priests bathed to purify themselves before the ceremonies.

The whole complex included everything that one would expect to find on a large estate. There were places for people to sleep, a school, a library, kitchens, granaries, a slaughterhouse, and storerooms. Beyond the walls lay many acres of farmland owned by the temple. Priests, scholars, musicians, and farm-laborers worked in the service of the god in these temples.

Karnak
The Temple of Amun at Karnak was the greatest and wealthiest temple in Egypt. This huge area of temples and buildings (1 × ½ mile) is now named after a nearby village, el-Karnak, but in ancient times it was known as *Ipet-isut*, "The Most Perfect of Places."

The ruins of the Temple of Amun seen from the southeast corner of the lake. The remains of the pylons, a columned hall and obelisks can be seen.

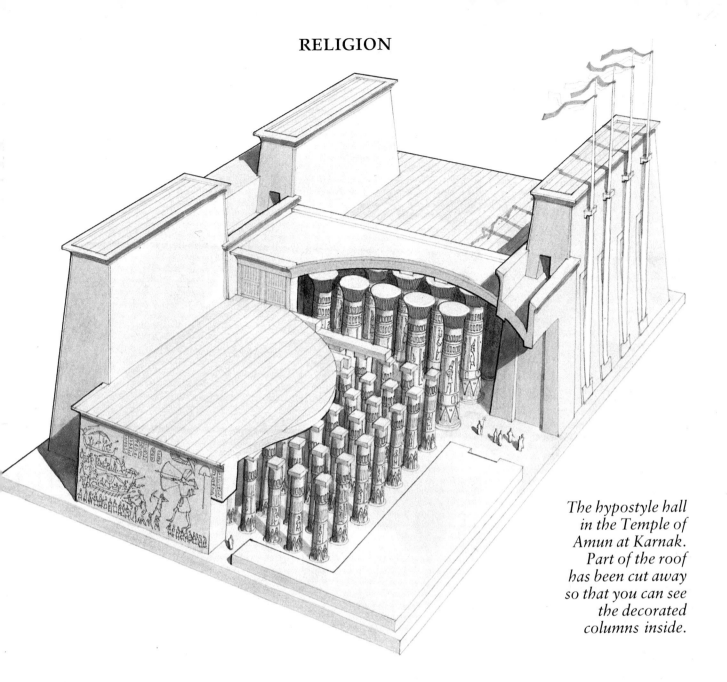

The hypostyle hall in the Temple of Amun at Karnak. Part of the roof has been cut away so that you can see the decorated columns inside.

When Thebes became the capital of Egypt, the temple of Amun grew in wealth and fame. Later it remained the most important religious center in the land. For 2,000 years the temples of this huge complex were continually being added to and restored.

An avenue of ram-headed sphinxes led from the quay to the first great pylon walls of Amun's temple, which stood in its own enclosure with other smaller temples, chapels and a sacred lake. Another avenue of rams ran from Karnak to the temple at nearby Luxor. Once a year there was a long religious festival, when the statue of Amun at Karnak visited the temple at Luxor.

The Great Temple consisted of a series of pylons built at various times, with halls between them, leading to the sanctuary, at the end of which was the shrine in which the statue of the god lived.

Beyond the second pylon lay the hypostyle hall (see above). Its 134 columns supported the roof and were shaped in the form of papyrus plants, representing the vegetation that surrounded the mythical island of Creation. On the exterior walls were reliefs of battles fought by the kings who had built the hall, Seti I and Ramesses II. To get some idea of the size of this vast hall, imagine that it is big enough to contain St. Peter's of Rome or the Cathedral of Notre Dame in Paris.

The New Kingdom

Hyksos domination

The history of Egypt during the Hyksos dominations is not well known. They ruled the north from their capital Avaris in the Delta. During this time many new developments and practical skills were introduced into Egypt. These included advanced methods of bronze-making, an improved potter's wheel, a vertical loom for weaving, as well as new fruits and vegetables. Certain medical instruments also date from this time.

Under Sequenenre' II the Thebans began their struggle to drive out the Hyksos. Kamose, Sequenenre's successor, almost captured Avaris and campaigned in Nubia. His successor, 'Ahmose, finally defeated the Hyksos and expelled them from the country.

The Colossi of Memnon are huge seated statues of Amenophis III (1417–1379 B.C.) which stood in front of his mortuary temple. Nothing else remains except a stela.

The 18th Dynasty

A new warlike spirit came into evidence, as a series of warrior kings won back the country's earlier frontiers and conquered a vast empire.

One of the officers who served under 'Ahmose, Amenophis I and Tuthmosis I described his career in the inscriptions in his tomb. Of the Syrian campaign he wrote:

> "... When his majesty reached Syria he found the foe marshaling his troops. Then he made a great slaughter of them. Countless were the living captives which his majesty brought back from his victories..."

Trade, tribute from foreign peoples and loot taken from enemies brought great wealth to Egypt. Some of this was buried with the Pharaohs who built their tombs in the cliffs across the river from their capital, Thebes. Great temples were built for the Theban god Amun, who now became the supreme god of Egypt. Amun's temple at Karnak became the greatest in the land and in time its priests became very powerful.

The reign of Queen Hatshepsut

Tuthmosis II (1492–79 BC) was succeeded by his young son, Tuthmosis III. Hatshepsut, Tuthmosis II's widow, acted at first as *regent*, but after two years she pronounced herself 'king' of Egypt. She ruled for 20 years. During this time there was little military activity and Egypt lost part of its empire in Asia. Hatshepsut's mortuary temple at Deir el-Bahri is one of the most beautiful buildings in Egypt (page 11).

When Tuthmosis III eventually came to the throne in his own right he tried to wipe out the name of Hatshepsut. Her monuments were desecrated and her name was obliterated from inscriptions. He then turned his attention abroad and in more than 15 campaigns he built an empire stretching from Syria to the Sudan.

This empire lasted until the end of the reign of his grandson, Amenophis III, who actively encouraged friendly relations with neighboring rulers. Luxurious living in a peaceful setting reached its climax during his reign and Amenophis III never campaigned abroad.

Akhenaten

His successor, Amenophis IV, was inspired by the idea that there was only one god, Aten, the sun disk. He took the name Akhenaten, meaning "beneficial to the sun disk" and moved the capital from Thebes to a new city (page 42).

Akhenaten's revolutionary ideas about religion were not popular. After his death, the young king Tutankhamun moved back to Thebes and the worship of Amun and the other gods was reintroduced. Tutankhamun died at the age of 20 but his successors did their best to eliminate all traces of the name of Akhenaten.

Akhenaten had been so busy with his religious reforms that he had had little time for other concerns. The powerful Hittites from the area we know as Turkey managed to gain control of Egypt's Syrian territories.

The 19th Dynasty

The early Pharaohs of the 19th Dynasty did much to restore Egypt's prestige. Seti I (1305–1290 B.C.) fought several campaigns in Western Asia and succeeded in regaining temporarily some of Egypt's Syrian possessions. His son, Ramesses II (1290–1224 B.C.), inherited his father's problems in this region. In the fifth year of his reign he fought against the Hittites at Qadesh. The results were indecisive but Ramesses presented it as a great victory in many temple reliefs.

After further battles during the next few years, there was a truce which was followed by a formal treaty. Peace continued for more than 50 years.

Seti I and Ramesses II carried out many building works and they moved the Egyptian capital to the Delta. Ramesses had many huge statues of himself carved and had his name cut on many earlier monuments. He became one of the best known of Egypt's rulers.

The 19th Dynasty eventually collapsed as rival princes struggled for the throne. The next ruling family produced only one great warrior king, Ramesses III.

Left: Amenophis I, the 18th Dynasty ruler who succeeded 'Ahmose, who had finally driven out the Hyksos rulers.

Below: Wall-painting showing Ramesses II shooting arrows at Nubians from his chariot. This was a popular theme and there are several pictures showing Ramesses in battle.

War and the Army

Until Egypt was invaded by the Asiatic Hyksos in about 1600 B.C., there was little need for a regular standing army. The country was well protected from invasion by the desert and the sea.

The Egyptians had no need to conquer other lands for food, as their own agriculture provided ample supplies. From time to time they sent expeditions to Sinai, for turquoise and copper, and to Nubia for gold and other precious objects. Soldiers accompanied these expeditions and were also needed when the desert tribes tried to move too near the fertile valley.

During the Middle Kingdom the Egyptians built a chain of fortresses in Nubia in the region of the Second Cataract and beyond. They housed large garrisons as well as scribes and other officials. Later in the New Kingdom, they were enlarged.

In the earliest times each district, or *nome*, had its own small army. Pharaoh's army consisted of soldiers from the nomes, who he employed whenever the need arose. The Pharaoh, who was the head of the army, had a royal bodyguard. Later some of them were mercenary soldiers from Nubia. Until the New Kingdom, the army consisted entirely of infantry, or foot soldiers, divided into light and heavy troops.

The influence of the Hykos

The Hyksos introduced the horse and light chariot into Egypt, which brought about a revolution in fighting methods. After the defeat of the Hyksos, the Egyptians attacked Palestine and Syria. A new regular army was established. The curved sword was added to the existing weapons of bows, spears, daggers, and axes. Armor also came into use.

The new army was organized into companies of 250 men led by a standard bearer. Strategy and tactics were developed. For example, according to official accounts, it was the plan of battle devised by Tuthmosis III that was responsible for his victory over Asiatic princes at Megiddo in c. 1455 B.C., although indiscipline of his new troops lost him the early part of the battle. Later, foreign mercenaries such as Nubians and Libyans formed an increasingly large section of the army.

The Pharaohs and their sons were in charge of the armies. There was a complex chain of command from generals and battalion commanders, to standard bearers and platoon leaders.

An Egyptian soldier carrying a spear, shield, and scimitar. The shield gave protection, although light body armor was introduced in the New Kingdom.

THE NEW KINGDOM

Tomb model of Nubian archers, dating from the Middle Kingdom. The Nubians were a warlike race and many fought as mercenary soldiers in the Egyptian army from c. 2000 B.C.

Increasing power of army officers

The standing army and the professional officers began to play an important part in the politics of Egypt. In the New Kingdom army officers became rich and powerful. The highest posts were open only to men who could read and write. They would begin as clerks in charge of accounts and stores and would then progress to general secretarial work, keeping the war diary and taking charge of recruits. Eventually they would be on the general staff.

The army was also a good career for adventurous young men, although the scribes liked to paint a miserable picture of the hard life of a soldier:

"... Come, let me tell you how the soldier fares with his many superiors ... Come, let me tell you how he marches over the mountains to Palestine. His bread and water are carried on his back like the load of an ass. His drink is foul water. He falls out only to go on picket duty. When he reaches the enemy he is like a pinioned bird and has no strength in his limbs. If he returns to Egypt he is like the worm-eaten wood. He is brought back upon an ass: his kit has been stolen and his servant has run off."

Egyptian weapons

1. Khopesh *or* scimitar: *Sickle-shaped sword for cutting and piercing. Of Asian origin and found in the New Kingdom.*
2, 3. Eye-ax *and* pole-ax: *Heads made of copper. Replaced the mace in the Old Kingdom.*
4. Dagger: *Sidearm used for hand-to-hand combat.*
5. Mace: *One of the oldest weapons, used in predynastic times. The stone head took various forms. Later replaced by the ax.*
6. Spear: *Used throughout Egyptian history; main weapon of the heavy infantry.*
7. Metal arrow heads
8. Horse-drawn chariot: *Made of wood, with some parts of leather and metal. It carried two soldiers: the charioteer and the chariot warrior.*

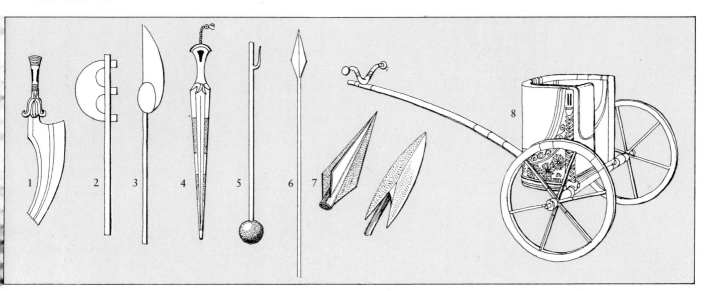

39

Neighbors

Until the end of the Middle Kingdom, most Egyptians had little contact with foreigners. The exceptions were those who were sent on trading expeditions or campaigns. From the earliest times, ships were sent to Byblos to obtain cedar wood and precious oils. In the Old and Middle Kingdoms expeditions went to Sinai to obtain turquoise and copper, and occasionally the Egyptians campaigned in Palestine and Syria. Nomadic or wandering Asiatics are sometimes shown on tomb reliefs, such as those trading eye-paint with a Middle Kingdom governor (page 24).

Nubians

More familiar were the Nubian people of Kush and Wawat where Egyptians went for gold and other precious objects such as ebony, ivory, animal skins, monkeys, and slaves. The Middle Kingdom rulers established forts with garrisons and later, during the New Kingdom, the region was again under Egyptian control. There were many Nubian mercenaries in Pharaoh's army and several tomb paintings show Nubians bringing him tribute.

Also to the south lay the land of Punt, which historians think may have been on the Horn of Africa or across the Red Sea where Yemen now is. From Punt came incense, which was used in vast quantities during religious rituals. On an expedition recorded on the walls of Queen Hatshepsut's temple at Deir el-Bahri, incense trees were brought back for replanting in the temple garden. They were carried in baskets to protect their roots. The roots of one of these trees can still be seen in the temple area of Deir el-Bahri.

Cretans

The Egyptians were also in contact with the Cretans, known to them as the Keftiu. Some Cretan pottery has been found in Egypt and Egyptian objects have been excavated in Crete, where a great civilization, called Minoan, flourished until about 1450 B.C.. Cretans in their distinctive garments and carrying pots, also appear in a tomb-painting.

Diplomatic visits

During the 18th Dynasty diplomats journeyed from Egypt to the land of the Kassites in Babylonia and to the Mitanni, in the area of North Syria and the Upper Euphrates. Letters were exchanged with distant Assyria. Through these

envoys, gifts were exchanged by the rulers. From Babylon came the precious gem-stone lapis-lazuli and the princes of Mitanni sent horses. In turn, Pharaoh provided gold.

We know about these contacts with distant neighbors because of a collection of royal letters found at Akhenaten's capital city, Akhetaten, now called el-Amarna. The letters were written in Akkadian, the language of the Babylonians, which was used for diplomatic purposes at that time. There were also letters from Canaanite princes of the Levant and Syria, which were by then under Egyptian control.

Far to the north, in Hatti, the Hittites emerged as a great power. The text of a truce between Ramesses II and the Hittite king is preserved on Egyptian temple reliefs, and in Akkadian on clay tablets from the Hittite capital Hattusas.

As time went by the Egyptians came more and more into contact with their neighbors.

Neighboring peoples with whom the Egyptians were in contact bringing gifts to the Pharaoh. From left to right: Syrians, Cretans, Nubians, and Babylonians. (Based on Egyptian and Babylonian wall-paintings.)

The Amarna Age

In the mid-14th century B.C. there was an extra-ordinary period in Egypt's history, known as the "Amarna Age." This was the reign of the religious revolutionary pharaoh, Amenophis IV, who abandoned the worship of Amun and the other traditional gods and replaced them with one god, the Aten, or sun disk. He changed his name to Akhenaten, meaning "beneficial to the sun disk" and moved his capital to a newly built city which he called "Akhetaten," "the horizon of the sun disk." This site, some 200 miles north of Thebes, is now called el-Amarna.

The cult of the Aten

At the beginning of his reign, Akhenaten gave himself the title of High Priest of the Sun god, a name which was traditional for Egyptian kings. As time went by the development of the cult of the Aten became the main purpose of his life.

At first Akhenaten tried to introduce the new religion at Karnak. Later he ordered that the temples of the other gods throughout the land be closed. When Akenaten then ordered that the name of the god "Amun" be hacked out of all inscriptions, the people must have been very angry. The powerful priests of Amun were also opposed to the new religion.

The wealth and power of these priests had already become a threat to the Pharaoh's authority. Akhenaten's father, Amenophis III, had taken measures against the priests by encouraging rivals to Amun. But Akhenaten worshiped the Aten with a zeal that went far beyond any possible political reasons.

Some people think that his fanatical devotion to the Aten was due to mental instability; others see Akhenaten as a prophetic visionary or an artistic genius. Certainly there were great changes in the

Wall-painting from the king's private residence at Amarna. It shows his two small daughters, the princesses Neferneferuaten-tasherit and Neferneferure, sitting together on a cushion. The picture is part of a much larger composition which included the whole royal family. The king and his wife had six daughters. During this period, the traditional rules of art were replaced by a realism that borders on caricature when people are represented, as can be seen from the princesses' elongated heads.

art of this period. We do not know whether the paintings and sculptures of the king show him as he really was or whether they are the result of new artistic developments. With his long gaunt face and female-shaped body. Akhenaten is made to look rather unusual. His wife, Nefertiti, appears to have been very beautiful.

The city of Akhetaten

At Akhetaten the king retreated into a world of his own making, away from Thebes and the hated Amun. Within two years of the new town being designed, the Pharaoh, his wife, children, officials and servants were able to move there.

The city was built in a narrow strip parallel to the river from which it was separated by cultivated fields. On the side facing the desert, wells were sunk for water. In the main city were the temples and palaces; to the north there was a suburb and a palace, and inland lay the workers' village.

When the royal family were not living in the beautifully decorated Great Palace, they spent their time at the Maru-Aten, a pleasure palace with a lake, to the south of the town.

The city was dedicated to the Aten in a ceremony recorded in boundary *stelae* or monuments. The most important building was the Great Temple of Aten. Here the sun god was worshiped at an altar under the open sky. There was music and singing and hundreds of offering tables were piled with flowers, fruit and food.

The Aten was thought to be the sole god from whom everything was created. Hymns were composed to the Aten:

"Splendid you rise in heaven's lightland,
O living Aten, Creator of life.
When you have dawned in Eastern Light-land
You fill every land with your beauty.
You are beauteous, great, radiant,
High over every land;
Your rays embrace the lands,
To the limit of all that you made."

Isolated from reality, Akhenaten neglected his country and its empire. He ignored requests for help from his dependents in Palestine. Farther north, Egypt's outlying provinces were attacked by the Hittites. At home, the cost of the new

Limestone relief found in the Royal Tomb at Amarna. It was probably a pattern for sculptors working on the chapel wall. Akhenaten, Nefertiti and two of their daughters play together.

capital and the Pharaoh's neglect of his duties, were causing unrest.

Disorder and unrest

There seem also to have been problems within Akhenaten's household, for Nefertiti retired in disgrace to a palace north of the city. Two years later Akhenaten died and the young prince Tutankhaten was proclaimed king. When Nefertiti died three years later, he went to Thebes, where the priests of Amun had reasserted their power, and his name was changed to Tutankhamun. He died young and his burial chambers remained intact until they were discovered in 1922 (page 84).

All traces of Akhenaten and the sun cult were wiped out. His name was desecrated and the existence of Akhetaten, the sun god's city, was forgotten. It was discovered by accident in 1887 and excavations began four years later. Since then, scholars have gradually built up a picture of the short-lived world of the mysterious Amarna Age.

Imperial Decline

Around 1200 B.C. the countries surrounding the Mediterranean were in turmoil. As you can see on the map, new groups of people appeared. Troy had fallen, as had the Mycenaean cities of Greece. The Hittite empire later vanished and cities of the Levant were destroyed. Egypt, like other countries in the region, was attacked by roving groups of raiders, known as the Sea People.

During the reign of Ramesses II's successor, Merneptah, a battle was fought against invading Libyans who were allied with the Sea People. The Egyptians defeated them, but under Ramesses III, Egypt was again attacked by the Libyans and the Sea People. Three campaigns were fought in the Delta and the invaders were beaten.

The campaigns of Ramesses III
The most serious threat occurred in the eighth year of the reign of Ramesses III, when he defeated the Sea People on land and at sea. He had his victory recorded on his great mortuary temple of Medinet Habu.

"The foreign countries made a plot in their islands... no land could stand before their arms, beginning with Khatti [the Hittites],... and Alasiya [Cyprus]... They came, the flame prepared before them, onward to Egypt... as for those who reached my boundary... their hearts and their souls are finished unto eternity... those who entered into the river mouths were confined... butchered and their corpses hacked up."

The picture below shows this great battle Ramesses' victories preserved the country from further invasion and Egypt was at peace for most of his reign. There were a few skirmishes in South Palestine, where one group of Sea People, the Peleset, settled.

Sea battle between Egyptians and the Sea People during the reign of Ramesses III. The Egyptians were victorious and saved the country from invasion. This relief is from the mortuary temple at Medinet Habu.

With peace abroad, the Pharaoh now turned his attention to trade and building works. His reign of 31 years was prosperous and he made many gifts to the temples.

Toward the end of his life, there were signs that all was not well. At one point, the monthly food rations paid to the workers on the royal tombs were overdue. This led to strikes which ended only when the vizier intervened. This was the first recorded strike in history.

Even more serious was the discovery of a plot to kill the Pharaoh. Many officials of the harem, the women's quarters, were involved, including several of the king's wives. The punishment for the plotters was not considered excessive for those times: some were permitted to kill themselves, while others had their nose and ears cut off.

The Ramesside Pharaohs

Under the next eight Pharaohs, who were all called Ramesses, Egypt lost the remnants of its empire and the country became more and more unstable. It was during these years that robbers plundered the royal tombs at Thebes (page 16).

During the reign of the last Ramesses, Egypt was virtually divided between the High Priest of Amun at Thebes and the Vizier of Lower Egypt, who ruled from Tanis in the northeast of the Delta. The Pharaoh withdrew to his residence in the Delta. Although he was still recognized as the Pharaoh, he no longer had any authority.

The struggle for power

Egypt's days of greatness were over. Rival kings ruled from different cities. At Tanis a line of kings descended from the vizier Smendes ruled for about 100 years, until 945 B.C.. At Thebes, the rulers were the descendants of the High Priest.

The Libyans, who had so frequently been repulsed when Egypt was strong, settled in the Western Delta and the Faiyum. They adopted the Egyptian way of life and many of their leading families became wealthy and powerful. For over 200 years these families controlled the Delta.

The country was in an unsettled state and Egypt's prestige among neighboring peoples sank. With so many different rulers within one country, it is hardly surprising that in due course, civil war broke out.

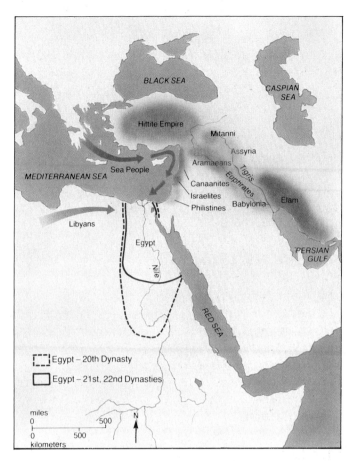

Map showing the position of the foreign powers surrounding Egypt at the time of the Ramesside Pharaohs.

The Victory Stela of Merneptah from his mortuary temple at Thebes shows Pharaoh between the gods and recounts his success against the Libyans and their northern allies. The battle took place in the western delta in year 5 of Merneptah's reign. The final portion of the stela praises the king's victories over all of Egypt's neighbors, including Palestine and Syria. For the first time "Israel" is mentioned in an Egyptian text.

Foreign Kings

"Now behold, thou trustest upon the staff of this broken reed, even upon Egypt, whereon if a man lean, it will go into his hand and pierce it; so is Pharaoh, King of Egypt, unto all that trust in him." (*The Bible: II Kings 18, v.21*)

This description of Egypt by an Assyrian describes how weak the country had become. By the middle of the 8th century B.C., Egypt was divided into a number of small states in the north, while the south was under the control of the High Priests of Amun. The loss of the empire had resulted in a decline in prosperity.

Egypt under Nubian rule

Nubia, for so long under Egyptian control, was now independent. Here, a dynasty of kings emerged who worshiped Amun and were on good terms with the Egyptian priests at Thebes.

After helping with a military campaign in the Delta, the Nubians became involved in Egypt's internal affairs and in due course became the Pharaohs of the 25th Dynasty.

For a while Egypt was relatively peaceful. Unfortunately the Nubians began to intrigue with the rulers of Palestine against Assyria. Under Sennacherib, the Assyrian king who devasted Judah in 701 B.C., the Egyptians only escaped attack when the Assyrian forces were struck down by a plague. It was this king's envoy who had called Egypt "a broken reed."

Assyrian rule

Sennacherib's son, Esarhaddon, did attack Egypt and forced the Pharaoh Taharqa to flee from Memphis. On the *stela* below Esarhaddon had the event recorded:

> "... Memphis ... in half a day, with mines, tunnels, assaults, I besieged, I captured, I destroyed, I devastated, I burned with fire ..."

He left no army, so Taharqa later returned.

In spite of the efforts of the Nubians to retain a unified kingdom, it was again broken up. The next Assyrian king, Assurbanipal, attacked not only Memphis but also Thebes.

> "Thebes in its entirety I conquered... silver, gold, precious stones, all the possessions of the palace... I took away from Thebes."

This was the end of the city's greatness. The Nubians returned to their country and the Assyrian king appointed *vassals* loyal to himself.

The Saite kings

Assyrian power declined and Egypt regained its independence under a dynasty of kings from Sais—the 26th Dynasty. This was a last great period of splendor in the Egyptian world.

These kings encouraged a revival of earlier forms of art and some beautiful objects were made at this time. They also began work on a canal to link the Red Sea with the Mediterranean and an expedition was sent to circumnavigate Africa.

The Saite kings established control over the Two Lands of Egypt and there was even an attempt to revive the empire of the New Kingdom. But there was a new power in place of Assyria. Under Nebuchadnezzar, who was later to capture Jerusalem, the Babylonians utterly defeated the Egyptians in 605 B.C.

Persian rule

The subsequent fall of Babylon to the Persian king Cyrus, in 539 B.C., gave Egypt another new neighbor. In 525 B.C. Cambyses, Cyrus's son, attacked and defeated Egypt.

Esarhaddon, the Assyrian King, had this stela *set up in Northern Syria. It shows the King with a* libation cup *in his right hand, from which he pours an offering to the gods symbolized at the top of the stela. In his left hand is a mace, a symbol of his kingship. From the left hand extend two ropes which pass through the lips of two figures at his feet. The first of these is Taharqa, whose hand and feet are shackled; he is on his knees, begging for mercy.*

The country was then ruled by a Persian *satrap*, or governor. The Persians were efficient administrators, regularly collecting taxes and governing Egypt mainly under its own laws. There were several unsuccessful revolts against the Persians. Finally, the Egyptians succeeded in driving them out, taking advantage of a temporary weakness of the Persians because of trouble in their capital.

The last Egyptian dynasties became more and more dependent on Greek mercenary soldiers, which imposed a heavy financial burden on the country. Egypt became unstable and the Persians again took control, in 341 B.C. Nine years later the Egyptians welcomed Alexander the Great.

Right: Map showing the foreign empires and kingdoms which took advantage of Egypt's weakness and came to dominate Egypt and the surrounding area.

Nubians bringing exotic objects from the southernmost region of the Empire to the king at Persepolis in Persia.

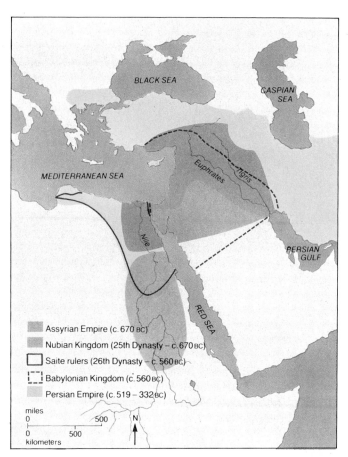

Assyrian Empire (c. 670 BC)
Nubian Kingdom (25th Dynasty – c. 670 BC)
Saite rulers (26th Dynasty – c. 560 BC)
Babylonian Kingdom (c. 560 BC)
Persian Empire (c. 519 – 332 BC)

miles
0   500

0   500
kilometers

N

Greeks and Romans

In 332 B.C. Alexander the Great took possession of Egypt without a struggle. He made plans for the building of a new city, Alexandria, in the northwest of the Delta on the Mediterranean coast.

Ptolemaic Egypt

After Alexander's death, his general, Ptolemy, took control of Egypt and brought Alexander's body there for burial. For the next 250 years Egypt was ruled by Ptolemy's descendents. Unlike previous foreign rulers, they did not rule the country as a part of another state but as an independent country.

Under the early Ptolemies there was progress in agriculture and commerce. The introduction of two harvests a year brought increased wealth to the country. Greek settlements grew up in many areas, particularly in the Faiyum, where land was reclaimed from the marshes.

Prosperity of Alexandria

Alexandria grew to become the leading city in the Greek world, although in many respects it was never really part of the Egyptian world. As it attracted more and more development, this hindered improvement elsewhere in the country.

One major reason for Alexandria's prosperity was the excellence of the two harbors that had been created by joining the island of Pharos to the mainland by a breakwater nearly a mile long. The two harbors were therefore positioned back to back; ships and traders from neighboring lands helped to turn the city into a bustling commercial centre.

The library of the city was the most famous in the world and attracted scholars from many other countries; there was a large Jewish community and it was here that the Bible was first translated into Greek, as this was now the language of the Jews of Alexandria.

Only in religious matters did the Alexandrians become part of the Egyptian world. The Ptolemies had deliberately started a new cult which included a mixture of Egyptian and Greek elements. Sarapis, the new god, was widely worshiped and was later one of the most popular of the Egyptian cults that spread to the Mediterranean world.

The coffin of Artemidorus with his portrait comes from Hawara in the Faiyum. It dates from the 2nd century A.D. and shows how the Greeks were influenced by Egyptian religion.

Egyptian traditions preserved

The Ptolemies appeared on monuments dressed as traditional Egyptian Pharaohs. They had some of their inscriptions written in Greek as well as *demotic* and *hieroglyphic*. It was an inscription preserved on the Rosetta Stone, dating from 196 B.C. in the reign of Ptolemy V, that enabled Champollion to decipher the Egyptian hieroglyphs (page 20).

Throughout the period of Greek rule, traditional Egyptian temples were built. It is likely that the Ptolemies deliberately encouraged building programs of this kind and continued to provide large incomes for the temples in order to gain the support of the priests, who were a powerful group.

Roman domination

For a time the Ptolemies controlled part of the Eastern Mediterranean but the expansion of Roman power to this region brought the two states into conflict. In 30 B.C. the Egyptian navy was defeated by the Romans; the Queen of Egypt, Cleopatra VII, and her husband, Mark Antony, died. The victor was Octavian, who later became the Roman Emperor Augustus.

Octavian treated Egypt as his personal possession, so that the country was ruled by a Roman official under the Emperor's control rather than by the Roman senate. In spite of increased prosperity through trade and agriculture, the Egyptians became poorer because the wealth was for Rome and not Egypt. Until the 3rd century A.D., 150,000 tons of grain were sent from Egypt to Rome each year. Ports were developed along the Red Sea coast and goods from the East passed through these on their way to Rome.

The Romans also absorbed elements of Egyptian culture, particularly their religious traditions. In Roman art there are several examples of the influence of Egypt.

The Egyptians later welcomed the arrival of Christianity, mainly because it provided an alternative to the customs and dominance of the Romans. Eventually the ancient Egyptian world and its traditions were lost under the influence of the Christian religion.

Above: Alexander did not use his own portrait on coins issued during his lifetime. His portrait was first used on coins of the Ptolemies. Here he is represented as Zeus Amun, wearing the ram's horns of the god Amun. He also wears a royal diadem, or crown. The Egyptians believed that all their Pharaohs were god-kings, so their image of Alexander was as a god.

Below: This mosaic of the first century A.D. is from the Roman town of Praeneste. It shows an Egyptian scene during the annual flooding of the river Nile.

Everyday Life

An Egyptian Village

Many villages in present-day Egypt are built on the site of ancient ones. They lie near the river but on high ground out of reach of the inundation. The mounds on which they sit are made even higher by the fact that centuries of mud-brick rubble have been piled on them. As one house fell down, another was built on top of it.

There is therefore little archaeological evidence of the earliest villages, especially as the decaying mud-brick has been used as fertiliser by generations of peasants. Whole villages have been lost in this way.

Most of the archaeological evidence for village life comes from the remains of villages built to house the families of craftsmen and officials working on the royal tombs. These villages, situated near the tombs, were in remote desert places. When the work force was no longer needed, the sites were abandoned. In time, they fell into ruin, but the sand which covered the ruins has preserved them.

Evidence for village life also comes from everyday objects found in tombs. In the Middle Kingdom models of entire houses were buried.

Most towns and villages in ancient Egypt grew up at regular intervals along the river. The villages were clustered near to the towns and, like them, they developed in an unplanned way, with houses joined on to each other. A warren of narrow streets divided blocks of houses. These villages probably looked much like those built on the same sites today.

Tomb-workers' villages

The tomb-workers' villages were different and were laid out to a plan, surrounded by walls to isolate the inhabitants from the outside world. The workers' village of Kahun was built in a slight hollow surrounded by cliffs, which made it easy to isolate the people. This village was built for the workers at the pyramid complex of the 12th Dynasty ruler Sesostris II, at Lahun in the Faiyum. Later it was inhabited by the priests who tended the cult of the dead king.

A tomb model of a granary. Men are loading the grain while a scribe records how much there is. This model was found in a tomb in Beni-Hasan and was made in about 1800 BC.

The houses were built of mud brick and most were one storey high, with stairs leading to the roof. Some rooms were plastered and gaily colored with red and yellow paint. The doors were made of wood. Workers and their families were grouped together by craft or trade. One important activity was weaving, which was done by both men and women. Spinning equipment and pieces of weaving have been found at Kahun, together with many objects of daily life.

El-Amarna

The workers' village at el-Amarna, site of Akhenaten's capital, was also laid out along straight narrow streets, within a boundary wall. The houses were cramped and small, being 16 feet wide and 30 feet deep, with four rooms. In all there were 72 of these cottages and a larger house for an overseer.

Deir el-Medinah

Life must have been far pleasanter in the village of Deir el-Medinah, home to the workers of the Theban royal tombs. Originally there was a single street with ten houses on either side, running back to an enclosure wall. Later the village was extended and at its largest there were 70 houses inside the wall and another 50 outside. This village was inhabited for three centuries. Nearby are the tombs and chapels of the craftsmen.

Typical houses

The houses were modified as required, to suit the needs of individual families. Animals had often been stabled in the front room at el-Amarna, but at Deir el-Medinah it came to be used as a household chapel for the family. On the wall, an image of the god Bes was painted and there were niches in the walls for offerings and statues of household gods. The yard outside was probably used as the kitchen area and there were cellars for storage.

Life in the workers' village

As the village was some distance from the tombs, the men did not return each night, but slept near the tombs in rough shelters, returning home at the end of each ten-day shift. There are a number of papyri and ostraca which help us to understand something of the lives of these workers and their families. The men were divided into two groups for their work, each with a foreman, his deputy, and one or more scribes. From time to time either the vizier or one of his officials visited the site to inspect the progress of the work.

Wages were paid in kind, usually with grain, given at the end of each month. Fish, vegetables, and sometimes meat, wine, and salt were also provided. It was in this village that the first recorded strike took place under Ramesses III when food rations were long overdue (page 45).

Above and below: Ruins of the tomb-workers' village at Deir el-Medinah in the Valley of the Kings. The village was built in the 18th Dynasty and was inhabited for over 300 years.

Typical house at Deir el-Medinah, with three main rooms and two cellars. The yard acted as a kitchen. The wall niches contained statues of household gods and family ancestors.

A Nobleman's House

Not all Egyptians lived in villages. Wealthy people had spacious and comfortable houses in large gardens on the outskirts of a town or in the country. At the site of el-Amarna, Akhenaten's specially built city, a nobleman's house has been excavated and gives a good picture of what these houses were like. Let us join an imaginary family in such a house.

A house in Akhetaten

Hor, his wife Tiy, and their four children have recently moved into their new house in the north suburb. Tiy had not wanted to leave their beautiful town house in Thebes, but as her husband is an important royal official, they had to obey the king's orders and move to Akhetaten.

Until their house was finished they had lived with a relative in the new town and the children had enjoyed watching the builders. Tiy chose wall colors and furnishings.

When the mud brick walls had been built, they were plastered and whitewashed. Large tiles were laid on the floor and painted in bright colors. Then wooden doors were installed.

The interior was painted in soft colours. The columns of the central hall were painted red and the rafters pink. Tiy chose a design of fruit and flowers for a frieze running along the upper part of the room. It is painted in the naturalistic style that is now fashionable.

Although she still misses Thebes, Tiy is delighted that the new house is so spacious. Apart from the central hall for entertaining, there is a smaller reception room, a small family room, several bedrooms, and a modern bathroom with stone-lined walls and floors and a lavatory. The roof quarters are cool and quiet and the view is superb.

Fortunately their cook is happy with the kitchens and even he has admitted that there is plenty of storage space and that the grain silos will be more than adequate. Flowers are already growing in the garden and the trees round the pool are growing fast.

Now that the furniture is in position, Tiy is feeling happier. Craftsmen have worked long hours to finish everything in time for the move. Apart from the usual beds, headrests, and stools, there are some delightful chairs with animal-shaped legs. Several chairs and some tables are inlaid with ivory and ebony.

Although they have brought some household utensils from Thebes, there are several new pieces. Tiy likes the painted pottery that is being made in the city.

Family life

The children are happy in their new home. The boys have made friends with the young grooms-man who lets them help with the horses and they can always be found either in the stables or the chariot house.

The girls like to play *senet* by the pool. At the moment however, they are playing with their wooden dolls on the shady roof terrace. They are taking it in turns to be Nefertiti and Akhenaten, while the dolls are the princesses.

Hor comes home from the palace; he hears the girls talking to their dolls, while the boys are pretending to do homework. He decides not to notice that they are really drawing pictures of horses instead, as he is feeling happy in his beautiful new home.

Typical furniture: a three-legged table, a stool, a low chair with the legs made to look like those of an animal and decorated with an inlay of ebony and ivory. A wine jar stands behind the table.

The house of a wealthy person stood in large grounds surrounded by a high wall. It was entered by a gateway, next to which was the gatekeeper's lodge. Sometimes there was a small temple or shrine nearby, for family worship. In this picture the gateway and lodge cannot be seen but they would have been in the foreground close to the shrine (a).

A pathway led to the house (b), which was built around a central hall. Here, the painted ceiling was supported by pillars and high up, close to the ceiling, there were several small windows with vertical bars. Against one wall was a low painted platform on which people sat on mats or low stools. Stairs led from the hall to the roof (c), where a light shelter provide shade and where there were cool breezes on hot evenings.

Outside there was a pool surrounded by trees and shrubs (d), reserved for the family and their guests. Within the walls of the estate there were rooms for the servants and estate workers (e), stables (f), sheds for other animals (g), storage rooms (h), and granaries (i), where the grain was kept. There was also a well (j) providing water for the household.

Eating and Drinking

The Egyptian daily diet

Egyptian wall-paintings frequently show the pleasures of the table enjoyed by the rich. But for the poor, the main foods were dried fish, bread, and vegetables. Various beans and lentils were also important and provided protein. The brown bean or *ful* is still widely eaten in Egypt. It is usually stewed slowly with onions and seasoning and is often accompanied by eggs.

There was little grazing land available for raising animals, so meat was expensive and most people ate it only on festive occasions. The cow was a sacred animal although beef was eaten occasionally. Goat and, to a lesser extent, lamb and mutton were also eaten.

Wildfowl and many types of game were hunted (page 56) and were popular. Domestic birds, including duck and geese, were raised and fattened for the pot. Fish had to be eaten soon after catching or it would spoil in the heat; often it was preserved by drying.

Eating and cooking

The rich soil of the Nile Valley provided an abundance of vegetables and fruits. These included onions, leeks, cucumber, radishes, melons, dates, and nuts.

There were many varieties of bread and cakes. Beer was made from barley and was drunk by the poor. Wine was kept in large jars and labeled with its date and origin. Fine wines were greatly enjoyed at banquets.

In large households the chef had several assistants. The equipment was simple and ovens were made of earthenware and fired by wood or charcoal. A door at the bottom allowed the air to flow and the ashes to be removed. Meat was grilled over an open fire or roasted on a spit.

A scene from Nebamun's banquet. Men and women usually sat separately. The guests wear cones of perfume on their heads, which melted during the evening and kept them cool.

Cooks preparing some of the many varieties of cakes. Flour was made from grain that was first pounded and then rubbed with stones. A little sand was sometimes added to make it finer, but this damaged people's teeth. Yeast, honey, milk, spices, and fats were other ingredients.

Wine was usually made from grapes, though other fruit was also used. After harvesting, the grapes were trodden in a large wine-press. The juice fermented in large earthenware jars which were later sealed. The vineyard and vintage were recorded on the jar-sealings.

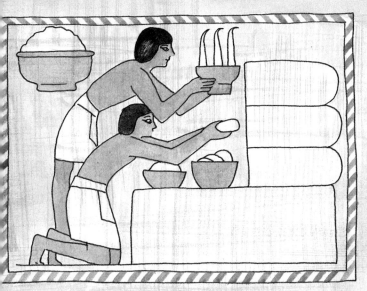

Collecting honeycombs from pottery hives. The combs were piled up in a bowl to allow the honey to drain out.

An ancient Egyptian recipe
The date palm grew wild in the Nile valley. In August this nutritious fruit was gathered from the trees and was often eaten fresh.

Here is a recipe for **date sweetmeats**. The date paste would have been made with a pestle and mortar, but nowadays it is easier to use a food blender, if possible.

Have a paste made for you in the blender, using 8oz. of dates and a little water. Add 1 teaspoonful of cinnamon and ½ teaspoonful of ground cardamom. Using your hands, work in 3½ oz. of coarsely chopped walnuts. Shape into little balls and roll in icing sugar. The Egyptians used honey for sweetener, so instead of icing sugar, you could roll the balls in honey and then dip them in finely ground almonds.

Hunting and Fishing

Nebamun's country estate

Nebamun and his family have come from Thebes to their estate in the Delta to enjoy a few days' hunting and fishing. Like many noblemen, this is Nebamun's favorite way of relaxing and escaping from the strains of court life and work.

Although he enjoys riding out into the desert with other noblemen to hunt ibex and antelope, he has recently noticed that his skill with the bow is not as good as it once was. In any case, he prefers spending his time with his family here in the Delta, where he grew up and learned to use the spear and throw-stick. Now that his sons are old enough, he will enjoy teaching them the pleasures of fishing and fowling in the marshes, where there are many varieties of fish and birds.

These few days are not only for pleasure. Recently, jackals have killed many of the ducks and geese on his farm outside Thebes and new breeding stock is needed. He and his wife are also planning to give a large banquet, for which many birds will be needed.

Nebamun has a large family and staff, as well as many household slaves and farmworkers and they must all be fed. While his estate produces enough food, extra game and fish from the Delta are always appreciated.

Fishing

To catch the large quantities of fish that will then be dried, the men use nets weighted with stones. A dozen men in two boats drop the broad and heavy rectangular net to the bottom of the river and then quickly raise it to stop the fish getting away. Any large fish are stunned with a mallet or a harpoon, which has a heavy wooden handle and a metal hook at the end.

Nebamun's young sons like to watch the fishermen working. One evening they went out with the men who were laying the bait to lure the fish from under the reeds. The men also laid down pots shaped like bottles, with bait placed inside, which were then hidden in the reeds. Next morning the boys went with the fishermen to see what had been caught. The pots were full. Downstream the bait had all been taken and landing nets were being used to haul the fish ashore.

The first fishing expedition

Even more exciting for the boys was their first day's fishing with their father. They were allowed to accompany him on a little papyrus boat. Under Nebamun's instructions, they quickly learned to use the spear and, with beginners' luck, even caught a few fish. Nobody told them that the catch was any smaller than usual, and Nebamun made little of harpooning a large fish. Later, the boys ate their own fish, grilled on charcoal.

Fowling

Today is the first fowling expedition, the best day of all. The boys are very excited and help to load the boats with decoys, throw-sticks and other equipment. They are to be on a boat with the gamekeeper and his helpers. Their father is on another boat with their mother and sister.

The sun has not yet risen as they board the light papyrus skiffs; last on are the cats, which are specially trained to chase and put up the birds for the hunters. It is the migration season, so there will be plenty of birds.

Soon the cats have put up ducks and geese, as well as snipe and teal and many birds that the boys cannot name. The sky is turning pink and is alive with the rush of wings; birds swoop and fall, the cats leap in and out of the papyrus thicket and on the boats the men hurl sticks at the birds and shout to one another. All is noise and confusion.

After a while the men begin picking up the birds they have killed and piling them on the skiffs, ready to begin counting them.

Hunting live birds

Later the children and their father go to examine the traps that have been set to catch live birds. The nets are stretched on wooden frames with hinged flaps. Bait is placed inside and the flaps are held open with strips of papyrus until the birds knock them as they enter the nets to take the bait. Several of the nets now have trapped birds inside them.

These birds will be taken to the farm for fattening and some will be sent to Thebes as breeding stock.

Nebamun hunting for birds in the marshes. He is holding three herons and a throw-stick shaped like a snake. His wife and young daughter are with him on his boat. Nebamun's cat has trapped three birds and everywhere there are birds and butterflies of all kinds.

Music and Games

Egyptian children and their parents had many games and leisure activities. As we have seen, men and boys enjoyed hunting and fishing, while women and girls sometimes joined family hunting expeditions, like the one described on page 56. Boys enjoyed games that tested their strength and skill; they ran, jumped, wrestled, swam, and played leap-frog. Throwing the javelin and target-practice with bow and arrow were popular with men and boys. There was also a sport which resembled fencing, where teams of boys fought each other with sticks.

Girls and boys played ball games with balls made of stuffed leather, vegetable fiber or painted wood. They also played with tops, marbles, and knucklebones, which were like an early form of dice. There were plenty of toys for quieter moments, such as dolls or wooden animals with moving parts (like the lion with the moving jaw in the illustration on page 59). Children also played with toy soldiers.

Older children and adults played board games. The most popular of these was called *senet*. The board for this game was rectangular and was divided into three rows of ten squares. The reverse side of the senet board is often found marked fo another popular game called *tjau* or "twent squares."

Festival processions

The Egyptians did not have theaters, but durin the festivals everyone watched the procession The Egyptians enjoyed music and dancing, whic were also a part of these festivities, in praise of th god. People also danced simply for pleasure, an professional dancers often entertained the guest at banquets.

A celebratory banquet

Let us imagine that we are guests at a banque sometime in the 15th century B.C. Our host is Theban nobleman who is celebrating his retur from Syria. Through dinner a blind harpist ha been playing his beautiful harp. As he plays, h sings an ancient song about life and death.

Musicians and dancers at the banquet. The girl or the left plays a double oboe. Next to her stand the lute player and the harpist. Another oboist sits with the girls, who clap to the music.

EVERYDAY LIFE

... Let not your heart sink
follow your heart and your happiness
Do the things on earth your heart commands
Make holiday
Do not weary of it
Lo, none is allowed to take his goods with him
Lo, none who departs comes back again."

Entertainment for the guests

Soon the dancing girls and their accompanists arrive, ready to begin the after-dinner entertainment. The musicians are all girls and are finely dressed; they wear scented cones of perfume on their heads, for it will be a long night and they must remain fresh. The harpist tunes her large standing harp and strikes the first chord. The dancing girls stamp their feet and clap their hands; the dance has begun.

Next to the harpist stands the lute player and she plucks the strings with a *plectrum*. The instrument's long neck is attached to a tortoiseshell soundbox, and everyone is delighted with the sound that the new lute makes.

Gradually the other players join in. The oboists play a duet and everyone claps and calls for more then the girls lay down their instruments. They oblige and start again. Slowly the tune begins to change. Three accompanists clap their hands gently and the harp and the lute strum quietly at first, then more persistently as the tambourine and drum join in. Finally the click of the wooden clappers and the sistrum are heard and the dancing becomes faster and faster. The girls whirl and spin; suddenly there is only the sound of the sistrum and the stamp of the dancers' feet; then silence, before the applause breaks.

Music and dancing in honour of Hathor

These dancers are the best in the city. Tonight, as always, they have performed in honor of Hathor, the goddess of music and dancing. The sistrum and the clappers (rather like castanets) are usually used for religious music. But this is a special banquet and the click of the clappers and the rattle of the sistrum make the perfect rhythmic sound for the end of the dance. It has been a memorable occasion and all the girls hope that their performance will be recorded in the tomb their master is preparing for himself.

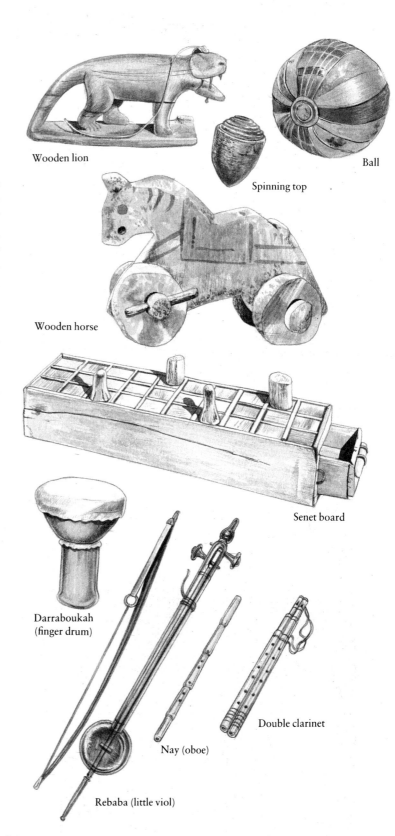

Wooden lion

Spinning top

Ball

Wooden horse

Senet board

Darraboukah
(finger drum)

Rebaba (little viol)

Nay (oboe)

Double clarinet

A collection of popular toys and instruments.

Clothing and Jewelry

Nofret, the daughter of a high official of Amenophis III is dressing for a banquet. Like many young Egyptian women, she is slender and pretty, with large dark eyes and short cropped hair. She has just bathed, assisted by her servants, one of whom now applies to Nofret her favorite lotus-scented cream to keep her skin soft. It is kept in a wooden perfume spoon.

Two of her maids are Syrian girls and they wear gaily-colored and embroidered dresses. Nofret is delighted to have a new delicately pleated robe with fringes, in the latest fashion. With a shudder, she thinks of the dreary, old-fashioned straight dresses that her grandmother insists on wearing.

First she puts on a fine linen undergarment, the shape of which is not unlike her grandmother's dresses. Her maid folds the robe around her waist and then pulls the two top corners over her shoulders, tying a knot under her breasts to keep it in place. Nofret is wearing her new red leather sandals. Usually she wears sandals of woven reed, but tonight is a special banquet.

1. *Bronze mirror with a handle made to look like a papyrus plant.*
2. *Spoon for cosmetics, made of calcite in the shape of a girl and a gazelle.*
3. *A glass jar containing kohl, which was used to make the eyes look larger.*
4. *A decorative comb with some of the teeth missing. (19th Dynasty).*

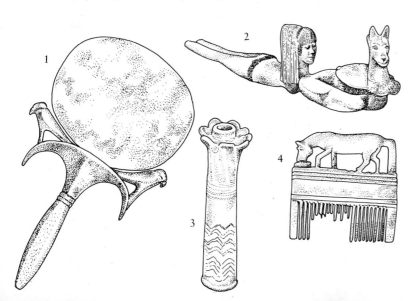

In the Old Kingdom men wore a knee-length kilt, knotted at the waist. Later, a longer kilt appeared tied at the chest and falling to below the knee. A sleeved, shirt-like garment also became fashionable. Women wore an ankle-length straight linen dress with straps or sleeves.
The people below wear the more elaborate New Kingdom fashions. Over a short underkilt, men wore long pleated skirts, knotted at the hips. The sleeves of the upper garment were also pleated. Women wore elegant pleated robes over the original straight garment.

Anat, one of the Syrian girls, is putting the finishing touches to the plaited wig, which is made of the best quality hair. Many girls have to wear dyed woolen wigs, but Nofret's father is a wealthy man and can afford this luxury for his daughter. Usually she wears combs of ivory or metal hairpins, but tonight she has decided that a few gold spangles would look prettier. When the wig is on, Anat ties a ribbon around Nofret's head and then inserts some flowers.

Nofret shuts her eyes so that a line of *kohl*, a black eye-paint, can be drawn along her upper lid. When it is dry, the maid draws another line under the lower lid, taking care not to smudge it, and extends it to make the eyes look larger. Nofret looks into the bronze mirror which her parents have given her and she now applies a little lipstick made of red ochre and resin.

Satisfied, Nofret puts the mirror down. She is soon to be married to Nahkt, who will be at the banquet, and she wishes to look her best.

Her younger brother and sister burst into the room. They start to tease Nofret, chanting some of the words of a song that Nahkt has asked the harper to sing for her:

"...the sister without peer, the handsomest of all... She looks like the morning star... Hair like true lapis-lazuli, arms surpassing gold, fingers like lotus buds..."

Jewelery

Nofret pretends not to hear, but in any case she is far too absorbed in choosing her jewels for the evening. She selects a collar of red, blue, and yellow stones, strung together to look like flowers; it even has green leaves. As it is a little heavy, it is supported at the back by a pendant. Recently, earrings have become fashionable and Nofret has had her ears pierced. She chooses plain-colored button-shaped studs, to match her collar. Then she puts on her gold bracelets, which are inlaid to look like turquoise and carnelian. Finally, she puts on armlets above her elbows and also anklets. Wearing all of these together is a new fashion and she knows that her grandmother will disapprove.

Her parents are waiting for her and they too are finely dressed. Her mother wears a *pectoral* of gold and precious stones which hangs from her beaded necklace. Nofret's father is wearing his gold collar and bracelets, given to him by the Pharaoh who is pleased with his official's work. He also wears a light cloak which is fringed and draped over one shoulder.

Everyday dress

Of course only wealthy people dressed like this. Most ordinary men and women wore much simpler clothing. Men wore kilts and women wore a straight robe. While working in the fields, men wore a loincloth. There are many wall-paintings and sculptures which show us how Egyptians dressed. In some museums you can even see Egyptian garments that have survived for more than 3,000 years.

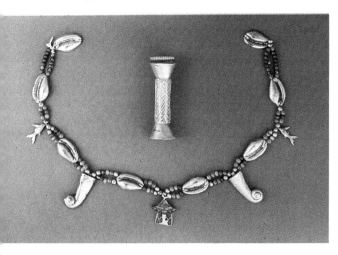

Above: (Top) Gold-sheet amulet case covered with granulation.
(Bottom) Necklace of silver cowrie-shell beads and beads of amethyst, lapis lazuli, carnelian, and feldspar, with amulets of fish, beards, and lotus flowers. (Middle Kingdom).

Below: Collar of glazed colored paste with rows of mandrake fruits, date-palm leaves, and lotus petals. (From the Amarna Age).

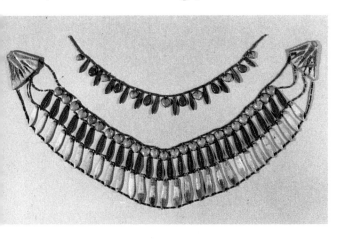

Crafts and Industry

Most of the best Egyptian craftsmen worked in the great temple workshops or in those attached to the palace or royal tombs. Others worked for noblemen who had workshops on their estates and there would probably have been some who worked in small towns and villages making objects to sell locally. Sons of craftsmen followed their father's trade and were trained by them from an early age.

There are many wall-paintings showing the highly organized state or temple workshops, where craftsmen worked under the care of a supervisor, who inspected all the finished products. Many different activities are shown in the wall-paintings and some are in the picture overleaf. Although they used simple tools, these skilled and patient craftsmen made objects of great beauty, some of which can still be seen in museums today.

Weighing metal

One important function carried out in the presence of an overseer was the weighing of metal. All metals were precious, as they were either rare or difficult to mine. Metals given to the craftsmen were weighed and the amount was carefully recorded. In the picture on the next pages you can see a man weighing metal; the scales have the feather of Ma'at on the top, to symbolize balance and fairness; the weight is made in the shape of a bull's head.

Goldsmiths

You can also see a goldsmith at work. He heats a small piece of metal in a fire. He holds the metal with a pair of tongs and blows through a blowpipe to raise the temperature in the furnace. Some metal objects were made by melting the metal and then pouring it into moulds of the desired shape, to harden. This was called *casting* and was used for small objects made of gold, though large bronze doors were also made in this way. Gold and other metals were also beaten into thin sheets, to be used for decorative purposes. Some were cut into fine strips and made into chains. Foil was wrapped around a cheaper substance to make attractive beads.

Bead-making

Semiprecious stones were also used to make beads; some of the most popular were turquoise, carnelian, amethyst, and the treasured lapis-lazuli from the east. The stones were broken up and roughly shaped by rolling. They were then smoothed by rubbing them together. To make holes for stringing them, a *bow-drill* was used. A piece of metal or stone was attached to the point of a stick which was turned by a bow string being pulled backward and forward. Once the holes were made, the beads were polished.

A colored glazed ceramic material, called *faience*, was also used to make beads as well as amulets and plaques to be placed on mummies. Faience was used to make plates, bowls, and drinking vessels.

Stone-working

From the earliest times stone-workers made fine vessels from the many decorative stones to be found in the hills and desert. They used saws to cut blocks of stone to about the right size formed into the right shape with a chisel or drill.

The sculptor used similar methods to make statues. Chisels were used to model the features.

The only surviving Egyptian map—a fragment of a sketch map that probably shows the quarries and gold mines in the central area of the Wadi Hammamat in the Eastern Desert.

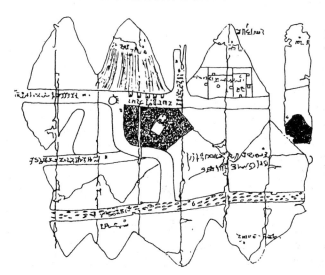

A preliminary drawing was used as the basis of reliefs and paintings. From the Middle Kingdom drawings of human figures were prepared within squared grids based on 18 squares from the ground to the hairline.
Left: Wooden drawing board with a grid marked for a drawing of Tuthmosis III. Trial hieroglyphs have been drawn on the right-hand side.
Right: A freehand drawing of a monkey and part of a seated figure on a squared-up ostraca.

which had been marked out with red ochre. Much patience was needed to make the huge granite statues. In the picture overleaf you can see sculptors putting the finishing touches to a sphinx.

Carpentry

The carpenters' methods were similar to those of today. In the picture you can see a carpenter making the leg of a table. The Egyptians had to import the best quality wood, such as cedar from the Levant, as their own woods were neither very good nor plentiful. Inlaid decorative patterns of ebony (a hard black wood) and ivory, were used to disguise poor quality wood.

Weaving and leather-work

Weaving was an ancient craft, known before the time of the Pharaohs. Cloth was made from flax. The linen fiber was beaten from the flax plant and then spun on a stick which was weighted with a flat or domed *whorl*. Many different types of cloth were woven on looms. Most cloth was plain, but Egypt was famous for its fine linens, some of which were almost transparent.

Rope, mats, and baskets were made of woven reed, grass or palm-fiber. Baskets were used for storage in the home. Some had lids and were used for holding linen or clothing. Small tables were also made from woven reeds. Sandals, too, were made of woven materials. In the picture you can see a man making sandals out of leather, which were worn only by wealthy people. Behind him a tanner is preparing animal skins which will be made into shields.

The scribes looked down on the craftsmen who worked with their hands and they wrote scornfully about them:

"I have seen the smith at work
At the opening of his furnace;
With fingers like the claws of a crocodile
He stinks more than roe fish.
The carpenter who wields an adz,
He is wearier than a field laborer
His field is the timber, his hoe the adz.
There is no end to his labor."

(*Satire of the Trades; Middle Kingdom*)

Farming

"In no country do they gather their seed with so little labor ..."

Herodotus

Farming was not quite so simple as Herodotus suggests and it required a great deal of hard work, but the abundant harvests and the ease with which crops grew made Egypt the envy of the ancient world.

Every year in late August and September the valley of the Nile was flooded. The soil was well soaked and a layer of fertile silt was laid down. Once the waters began to fall in October, the farming year began.

The fields had first to be put back in order and their boundaries re-established. The dikes and irrigation channels were repaired and any heavy soil was broken up with hoes.

Plowing and sowing

Plowing and sowing took place at the same time. The plow was pulled by cows and was guided from behind by the plowman. The sower scattered the seed in the furrows and it was then trodden in by animals. Sometimes the seed was scattered first and the plow was used to push it into the ground.

While the crops were ripening they had to be watered. A network of canals crossed the culti-vated land. Water was led into the fields along small irrigation ditches. The plants also had to be weeded and protected from pests.

Shortly before harvest-time, tax assessors came to estimate the likely crop yield and to fix the amount of tax the farmer was to pay.

Harvesting

When the crop was ready, the men harvested the grain using short curved sickles. They cut the grain just below the ear, leaving the straw to be cut later. This was used for animal feed, basketry, and brick-making. The grain was put in large baskets and carried on poles by pairs of men to the threshing floor. Here, oxen trampled the grain to separate the corn. Winnowing fans were used to toss the grain high into the air so that the chaff was blown away and the wheat fell to the ground.

The harvest was then recorded and the tax was collected. The grain was taken for storage in granaries. Offerings were made to the goddess of the harvest, the cobra-headed Renenutet. (In the picture on page 67 and on the back cover of this book you can see a harvest taking place.)

Wine making

Grapes were cultivated for wine and were har-vested by hand. They were then placed in vats

The cattle inspection. Large herds of cattle were reared for meat, dairy produce, for ritual sacrifice, and as beasts of burden. Here, a herd of long-horned, short-horned and hump-backed cattle are being brought for inspection by the owner of an estate. Large herds were reared on temple lands as well as on royal and noble estates.

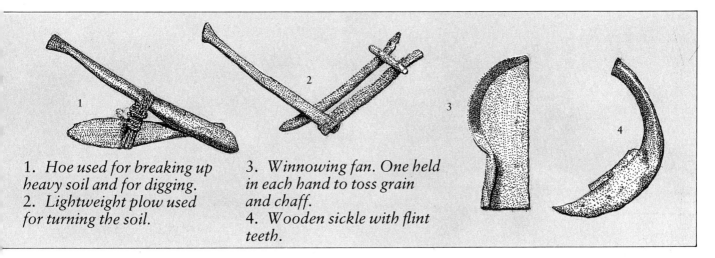

1. *Hoe used for breaking up heavy soil and for digging.*
2. *Lightweight plow used for turning the soil.*
3. *Winnowing fan. One held in each hand to toss grain and chaff.*
4. *Wooden sickle with flint teeth.*

where men crushed them with their feet. The juice was put into open pots to ferment. Later, the wine was poured into jars which were sealed and labeled. Cattle were bred for meat (a luxury for most people) and for dairy products.

The farming skills of the Egyptians were described by the Greek historian Doidorus:

"They far excelled the husbandmen of other countries and had become acquainted with the capabilities of the land, the mode of irrigation, the exact season for sowing and reaping ..."

The harvest. Corn was cut just below the ear with sickles. Later the straw was cut. In the foreground, men place the grain in baskets to be taken to the threshing floor.

Medicine and Doctors

The international fame of Egyptian doctors

The doctors of Egypt were highly regarded in the ancient world. Apart from the references to Egyptian medicine by Greek authors, there is evidence of their reputation much earlier, when the court physician of Amenophis II cured a Syrian prince. The Persian kings Cyrus and Darius preferred to employ Egyptian doctors and, as ruler of Egypt, Darius ordered the restoration of the medical school in Sais.

Egyptian doctors had a good understanding of anatomy. This was partly due to a long tradition of dissecting animals for sacrifice. But more importantly, they had learned about human bodies from the process of mummification, when the vital organs were removed from the body (page 74).

Remedies and treatment

There are many remedies and treatments recorded in medical papyri. In one of the most famous, known as the Edwin Smith Papyrus, there is a description of the way the heart works. Although it does not describe the circulation of the blood, the pulse points are recognized.

This description is followed by 48 surgical cases, each describing the illness, diagnosing it, forecasting what is likely to happen and then prescribing treatment. These are what doctors today would call *clinical observations*. The text ends with a series of magical spells and prescriptions for making old people look younger.

Medicine and magic

Medicine in Egypt was a combination of rational science and magic. Wounds or ailments that could be seen were treated practically and efficiently, while some less obvious illnesses were often thought to be the work of hidden evil forces. In these cases *amulets* and ritual spells formed part of the treatment. Amulets were small charms placed on the patient's body to ward off evil spirits.

There were three types of doctors—the surgeons, the priest-doctors, and the magicians. Doctors were often the priests of Sekhmet, the goddess of healing.

The treatment of wounds and visible ailments was advanced for its time. Many of the procedures described in the papyri for the examination and treatment of the patient are little different to those used today. Deep cuts were stitched and fractures were splintered and bandaged. Operations were carried out with the patient under sedation from a drug such as opium.

The medical texts show that there was an attempt to place illnesses into categories. The Egyptians understood the importance of hygiene and cleanliness for preventing certain illnesses and

Modern X-ray equipment explores the remains of the body inside the wrappings of a mummy. Evidence for the diseases suffered by Egyptians has been obtained in this way.

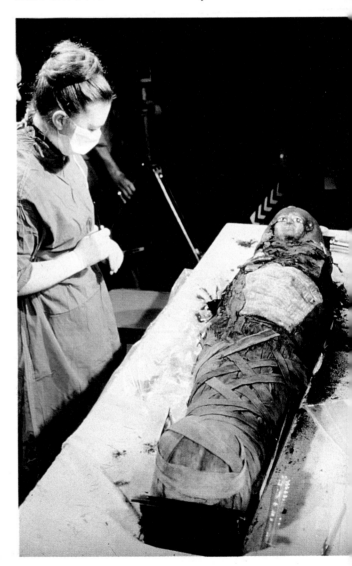

were well aware of the need for a patient to rest in order to recover.

The doctors' knowledge of natural drugs from plants was considerable. Herbs were picked on certain days and under particular conditions. Onions, coriander, cumin, dill, figs, and castor oil were all used for medicinal purposes. Minerals were also used, such as copper salts as an antiseptic. The prescriptions give precise details of the dosage, when it is to be taken and for how long, according to the age of the patient.

Doctors at work

Let us imagine two different kinds of doctors at work. The first performs a complicated operation known as *trepanation*, which was not a widespread practice, as it demanded a high degree of skill; the second uses a combination of medicine and magical rituals.

... It has been an unhappy few months for Nahkt and his family. First, his elder brother Khety had been badly injured while on an expedition to the "Turquoise Terraces," in the desolate mountain valleys of Sinai. His first assignment after promotion in the army was as an assistant to the "Chief of the North Lands." Under this official, he had helped to lead 750 men to the turquoise mines.

On the return journey a small band of nomads had attacked them and Khety had received a severe head injury. He was lucky to be alive and owed his life to the skill of a young surgeon. Khety had been drugged and then a portion of his skull that was pressing on his brain had been removed with a saw and knives. Afterwards the bone had been replaced and his scalp sewn up. The muscles on one side of his body are still paralyzed, which makes him limp.

Apart from Khety's injuries, both he and Nahkt are worried about their youngest brother, Senmut. He has never been very strong and his coughs and fevers have suddenly become worse and worse, in spite of the family's prayers and offerings to Sekhmet. The doctor has been trying several medicines and has recited spells over an amulet which he placed on Sekhmet's body. The prayers and chanting continue as everyone wills the little boy to live.

Modern-day medical interest

Nowadays scientists and doctors examine Egyptian mummies to discover the cause of death. The mummies are sometimes X-rayed or they are carefully cut open. Various illnesses have been diagnosed, including appendicitis and tuberculosis. Although the Egyptians could not usually cure such illnesses, their medical skills were far in advance of many later peoples.

Surgical instruments used by Egyptian doctors. The case is made out of cane and papyrus and was used by doctors for carrying their instruments.

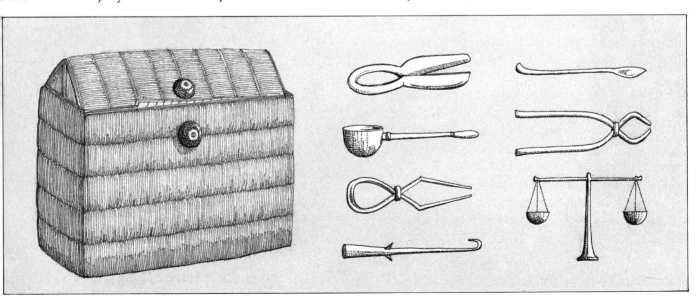

The Scribes and Literature

"Set your sight on being a scribe; a fine profession that suits you. You call for one; a thousand answer you. You stride freely on the road. You will not be like the hired ox. You are in front of the others."

Papyrus Lansing: 20th Dynasty

The profession of scribe was highly regarded in Ancient Egypt, not least by the scribes themselves. There are many surviving texts describing the pleasures of the scribe's life compared with that of the soldier or farmer. Some of these survive because they were copied by generations of pupils studying to become scribes and were passed on from one age to the next.

Although the rewards of being a scribe were great, the training could take as long as twelve years. All the high offices of state, whether in the palace, the treasury, the temple, or the army, were filled by men who could read and write.

The work of a scribe

Many scribes were civil servants who kept records and accounts and wrote letters, reports, and legal documents. They kept the machinery of government working. Others were more scholarly and wrote mathematical or medical papers. Some acted as teachers or librarians, working in "The House of Life" (the writing center of the temples) copying books and composing inscriptions.

Those who were not so well educated worked in the villages, writing letters and documents for people who could not write themselves and reading for them.

Apart from these activities, some scribes produced works of literature. These included poems, stories, hymns, and other types of books. Although we do not know the names of the original authors, we know that generations of Egyptians enjoyed these stories.

Here is a typical example:

The Story of Sinuhe

"On the seventh day of the third month of the inundation in the 30th year of his reign, the god ascended to his horizon. The King of Upper and Lower Egypt flew to Heaven and united with the sun disk ... Then the palace

Below: The scribe's writing equipment consisted of a palette, a water pot, and a brush holder. A thin reed with a frayed top was used as a brush, although this was later replaced by a stylus—a reed with a sharpened point. Hollows in the palette held cakes of red and black ink. Texts were written in black and red was used for headings and for emphasis.

Right: A limestone statue of a scribe, found in Saqqara and dating from the 5th Dynasty.

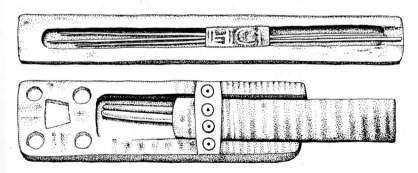

was hushed; hearts grieved; the great gates were shut; the courtiers bowed their heads and the people moaned ..."

King Amenemhet has died and Sinuhe, who was one of his courtiers, is now worried about what will happen in Egypt. He flees to Palestine and there becomes friends with a local prince whose daughter he marries. They have a family and he is very happy.

"... It was a good land called Yaa. Figs were in it and grapes. It had more wine than water. Abundant was its honey, plentiful its oil. All kinds of fruit were on its trees ... I passed many years, my children becoming strong men, each a master of his tribe ..."

But trouble interrupts this peaceful life. Sinuhe helps the prince against enemy tribes and defeats a strong man in single combat. As he gets older Sinuhe longs to be at home, so that he may die in his own country and have a proper Egyptian burial. Finally he returns, is welcomed by the new king and pardoned for his flight.

"I was clothed in fine linen; I was anointed with fine oil. I slept on a bed ... I was given a house and garden ... a stone pyramid was built for me ..."

The story goes into great detail about his journey to Palestine, the people he met on the way, his life away from home and his happy return. It was a very popular tale and was copied and recopied many times.

The Report of Wen-Amun

This is from a later period and tells of the difficulties Wen-Amun experienced on his journey to the Levant. He has been sent to buy cedar wood for Amun's sacred boat. Everywhere he goes he is badly treated; pirates rob him and the prince of Byblos refuses to help him. Finally he arrives in Cyprus, where we have a last glimpse of him talking to the princess who appears to be merciful, but here the story breaks off.

We can see how highly regarded the writers of poems and stories were from these lines written about them by a later scribe:

"... their tombstones are covered with sand, their chambers forgotten. But their names are pronounced because of the good books they wrote and their memory is for evermore."

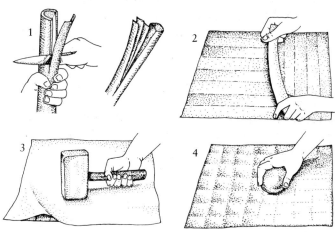

Papyrus making

Papyrus writing material was made from a marsh reed of the Nile called papyrus (top).

(1) After the stalks were harvested, the bark was peeled off and the stem was cut into pieces measuring about 12 inches in length. These pieces were then sliced lengthwise from the pith.

(2) The strips were laid on a cloth, side by side and overlapping slightly. More strips were laid over these at right angles.

(3) Another cloth was placed on top and the strips were beaten with a mallet. The pounding action made the strips stick to each other. The resulting sheet of papyrus was slightly sticky and was put out to dry in the sun.

(4) It was then rubbed smooth with a stone or a piece of wood. Long rolls were formed by sticking the edges together with a paste made of flour and water.

Education

"O scribe do not be idle... or you shall be cursed straightway. Do not give your heart to pleasure or you shall fail. Write with your hand, recite with your mouth... Do not spend a day of idleness or you shall be beaten. A boy's ear is on his back and he listens when he is beaten..."

Advice to the youthful scribe (Papyrus Anastasi)

Most of the boys who went to school were sent there to learn to be scribes. Many Egyptian children did not go to school, but went to work with their fathers and learned his trade. Girls stayed at home with their mothers and were taught household skills, although there is evidence that some girls were taught to read and write.

Reading and writing were essential for anyone who was going to be a state official. For nearly all the professions, including medicine and the priesthood, boys had first to train as scribes so that they could read the text books. Most boys learned the same profession as their father.

Temple schools
Schools were attached to the temples, although noble boys sometimes went to school at the Palace, where they were taught with the royal children. Sometimes boys were sent away from home to attend a particular school.

The children were taught in groups by teachers who were very strict and made their pupils work hard. Boys who misbehaved or were lazy were often beaten.

There was a lot of learning by rote and the boys began by learning by heart the different picture-signs grouped into various categories. As they progressed, they practiced writing model letters and exercises, and copies of the classics. They learned to read by chanting.

A day at school
Nahkt lives in Thebes and goes to school in "The House of Life" which is part of the great temple complex of Amun. He is a little late this morning and his teacher, an elderly scribe, has given him a punishment. He must copy out the "Advice to a youthful scribe" before he can go home.

Sighing, he fetches his writing equipment and sits on the floor with the other boys. Next to each boy is the scribal palette with red and black ink and a water jug in which to dip the reed brush. Most of them write on *potsherds*, although a few are using wooden writing boards. These have a prepared surface and can be washed clean and re-used. Nahkt's writing is still very untidy and until it improves he must use potsherds.

The teacher has now selected a papyrus scroll for dictation and waits impatiently for Nahkt to be ready. He stands up, flicks his cane as a warning to them, and begins "... Set your sight on being a scribe..." Nakht has heard it so many times before that he knows it by heart. He also knows that he is still making mistakes.

Learning hieroglyphs
When they have finished, the boys hand in their work for correction. Next, they are given some difficult signs to practice. Several times Nahkt reaches out for the rag which he uses to rub out mistakes. He wishes now that he had not spent yesterday afternoon wrestling with friends when he should have been doing his homework.

Learning to be a scribe is difficult, for there are so many signs to remember. Nahkt doubts that he will ever be good enough to write on papyrus, let alone the writing board. Papyrus is expensive, so only the experienced older boys may write on it. Although Nahkt can read most of the hieroglyphs he is bad at drawing them.

Reading aloud
After break they are given papyrus scrolls to read aloud. This time they all sigh, for it is a boring text reminding them of the scribe's superior status. They begin to chant "... I have been told that you have abandoned writing and that you reel about in pleasures... that you have turned your back on hieroglyphics". By now they all wish that they could.

Right: Schoolboys wrote on potsherds *or limestone flakes, called* ostraca. *They used a scribe's palette and brush. The younger boys in the background wear their hair in the "lock of youth."*

The Land of the Dead

Mummification

There are many mummies in museums all over the world. Perhaps you have seen one and wondered why the Egyptians mummified their dead. So many mummies and objects from tombs have been found that people often think that the Egyptians were obsessed with death. In fact, their belief in a life after death was the result of their enjoyment of life and their desire to continue life's pleasures in the next world.

The Egyptians believed that if everything was properly arranged, the dead person would live on in the Other World. They believed that when someone died various spirits were released. The most important of these were the *ka* and the *ba*.

The ka and ba spirits

The *ka* was the life force, created at the same time as the body. At death the ka stayed attached to the body and looked after it, living in the tomb inside the funerary statue. The human-headed *ba*-bird symbolized the individual personality of the living person. During the day it visited the world of the living and at night it returned to the tomb.

It was essential for a dead body to be properly preserved in a recognisable form if the ka and ba spirits were to survive. Without these spirits the dead person could not exist in the after life. It was for this reason that the Egyptians mummified their dead.

Early burials

In the earliest days of the Egyptian world, the dead were buried in the sand. This dried out the body before it had time to decay and so preserved it naturally. When more elaborate brick tombs began to be built, the bodies decayed because they were no longer in contact with the hot, dry sand. Various methods were tried to make the body look alive so that the spirits would survive.

At first, resin-coated bandages were wrapped round the body and the face was painted on the outer wrappings. Later, a chemical method was developed for drying and preserving the body. This is the process called mummification.

The well-preserved body of Seti I, found in the royal cache of mummies at Deir el-Bahri, Thebes.

THE LAND OF THE DEAD

The work of the embalmers

Originally only high-ranking people were mummified. Later the practice spread. There was a huge industry devoted to preparing bodies for tombs. There was even a scale of charges for mummification, ranging from the simplest to the most elaborate.

After death the body was taken to the funerary workshops on the west bank of the river. First it was washed. Then the vital organs—the heart, lungs, liver, and intestines—were removed, together with the brain. The heart was later returned to the body but the other organs were placed in *canopic jars*, which were put into the tomb with the coffin and funerary goods.

The mummification process

The body was covered with natron (a compound of sodium and carbon) for 40 days, to dry it out. After this the body was washed and packed with resin-coated bandages and bags of fragrant spices. Then it was bandaged and adorned with *amulets* and jewels. A painted mask went over the face and it was bandaged again.

Meanwhile the coffins had been prepared. These varied in design, but usually there were three, which were shaped like bodies and fitted into each other. They were painted inside and out with magical texts and illustrations. Finally the mummy was placed inside the nest of coffins and they were all put in a large outer coffin.

The embalmers' workshop.
Here the body was prepared under the supervision
of specialist priests.

Funerals and Burial Equipment

Burial equipment

1. Shabti box: *painted wooden box containing shabti figures. From the tomb of a Theban princess.*

2. Shabti: *From the end of the Middle Kingdom, one or more of these statues formed part of the burial equipment. They were the dead person's substitute workers and carried appropriate tools.*

3. Amulet: *formed from three symbols—the* ankh *sign of life, the* djed *pillar for fertility, and the* was *scepter, symbol of happiness.*

4. Winged scarab amulet: *placed in the mummy wrappings.*

5. Scarab beetle or kheper: *the sacred beetle was the symbol of creation and regeneration. The Egyptians believed it created itself.*

6. Pectoral plaque: *with winged* udjat *eye, symbol of the power of the god of light; it was also used as protection against the evil eye. The jackal is Anubis, the god of the dead and of embalming. Funerary priests sometimes wore a jackal's head when tending the mummy.*

7. Model boat: *in the Middle Kingdom non-royal burials were equipped with wooden models showing servants performing various tasks for the tomb's mummy.*

Wall painting showing the soul of the dead person rowing his boat across the river, crossing to the Other World.

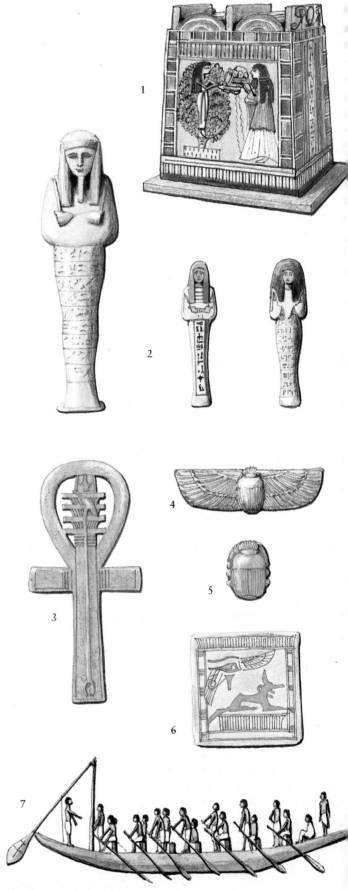

THE LAND OF THE DEAD

The funerary procession

On the day of the burial, the funerary procession crossed the river and fetched the mummy to take it to the tomb. The mummy was placed in a booth, shaped like a shrine and decked with flowers. It was mounted on a boat-shaped frame, or *bier*, and drawn on a sled by oxen. The widow sat beside the bier and the mummy was attended by two women mourners, who represented the goddesses Isis and Nephthys.

In front walked a priest, waving a censer and sprinkling milk. Behind the bier walked the important guests. They were followed by a small sled on which was placed a chest containing the *canopic jars*. In the procession there were also professional mourners. These women, dressed in blue (the color of mourning), were paid to wail and scream and to tear their hair. A long procession of servants carried the funerary goods and furniture to be placed in the tomb.

Burial equipment

Wall paintings and papyri show that these processions were an impressive sight. There were tables piled high with food and flowers and jars of wine for the feast after the burial. Then there were all the dead person's possessions that would go into the tomb: chairs, tables, stools, beds, and headrests, linen, boxes and chests, clothing and jewelry, games, jars of wine, and food.

There were also boxes of *shabti figures*, the little statues who would do the dead person's work. In the Other World was the Field of Reeds, where the grain grew tall and the trees bore great quantities of fruit. The dead had to plow and sow and reap, to keep everything in order. The shabtis were the servants who did this work for the dead.

Magical objects for burial and ritual implements for the last rites were carried in the procession. There were also men wearing kilts and tall white head-dresses who danced and clapped their hands above their heads. The *Reader-priest* recited prayers and spells.

Opening of the mouth ceremony

Once the tomb had been reached, the most important ceremony took place. This was called the *Opening of the Mouth*, which gave back to the mummy all the functions that had been lost at death. Only then could life be enjoyed in the next world. The mummy was propped up in front of the tomb chapel and the Sem-priest, acting as the dead person's son, used various ritual implements to perform the ceremony. The face of the mummy was touched and offerings were made. The mummy was then placed in its nest of coffins.

The final rituals

A copy of the *Book of the Dead* was placed in the coffin. This book was written on papyrus and illustrated with small pictures. It was a list of some two hundred spells to help the dead pass through the dangers of the Underworld before reaching the paradise of the Other World.

Once the mummy and all its belongings were in position, the tomb could be sealed forever. Any weapons which might harm the dead were broken ritually. Magic figures and bricks were set around the coffin and the door was sealed. The mourners then ate the funerary feast outside the tomb.

The ceremony of Opening the Mouth was carried out on the mummy in front of the tomb. The ritual was intended to restore to the mummy its five senses by means of a magical act.

Pyramids

During the Old Kingdom, Pharaohs began to be buried in huge tombs that we call pyramids. The first of these was built for Djoser by the architect and vizier, Imhotep. It is at Saqqara, the burial site near Memphis, and is called the *step pyramid* because of its shape. It began as a *mastaba* or bench-shaped tomb and was modified six times to become a pyramid of six steps.

There were various shapes before the step pyramid developed into the *true pyramid*. One experiment was the *bent pyramid* of Snofru at Dahshur, where changes were made to the angles of the side.

The pyramids at Giza

The pyramids of the 4th Dynasty Pharaohs at Giza were the largest of all. They were the most carefully built and are the best preserved. Khufu's Great Pyramid is made of more than two million blocks of stone. It was completed towards the end of his 23-year reign. This means that every day, 285 blocks, each weighing about 2½ tonnes, were quarried, prepared, transported to the site, and set in place.

The outer casing was of fine white limestone and the pyramid was topped by a golden capstone. A well-preserved wooden boat was found buried next to Khufu's tomb and was probably used to carry the Pharaoh's body.

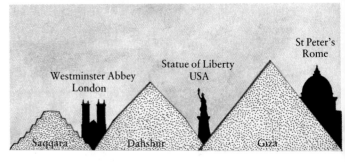

Left to right: step pyramid of Djoser at Saqqara (3rd Dynasty); bent pyramid of Snofru at Dahshur (4th Dynasty); Great Pyramid of Khufu at Giza (4th Dynasty), compared with other large structures.

Later pyramids were smaller; some were filled with rubble and others were built with mud-bricks. Pyramids were built at the desert's edge on the west bank of the Nile. The burial area was situated either inside the pyramid or below the ground and there were several chambers designed for the Pharaoh's use in his eternal life. A causeway connected the pyramid to the river.

Attendants brought the Pharaoh's body and all his goods by boat to the pyramid complex. After landing, the procession entered the *valley temple* and religious rituals were performed. The procession then went along the causeway to the *mortuary temple* for the funeral rites before the body was buried in the pyramid. Priests chanted magical spells so that the Pharaoh could join the sun god Re' in the sky. The boat was buried within

The pyramid complex of Djoser at Saqqara

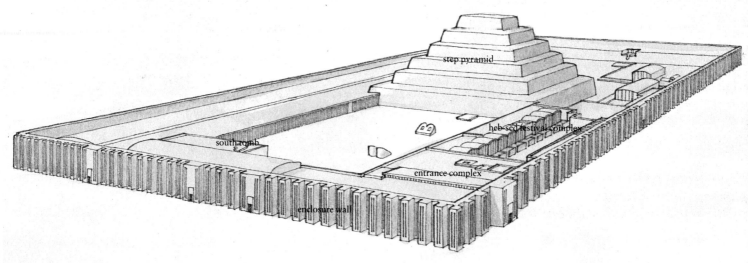

step pyramid

heb-sed festival complex

south tomb

entrance complex

enclosure wall

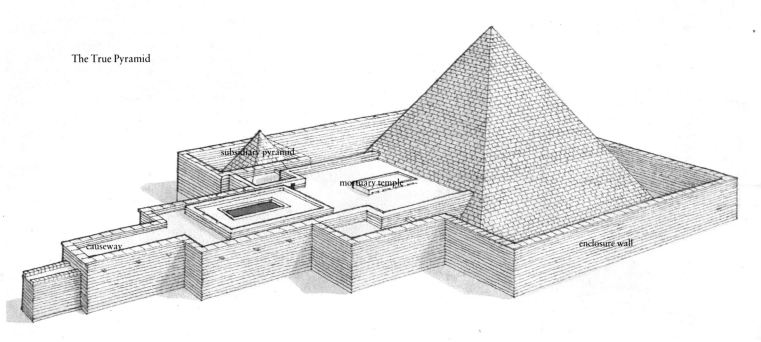

The True Pyramid

subsidiary pyramid

mortuary temple

causeway

enclosure wall

the pyramid complex, possibly for the Pharaoh to use when he sailed around the sky.

There are inscriptions in some of the pyramids which were magical spells, known to us as the "Pyramid Texts." For example:
"A ramp to the sky is built for him, that he may go up to the sky on it... he flies as a bird, and he settles as a beetle on an empty seat that is in the ship of Re'."
The ramp was probably the pyramid and the magic cast by the spell was believed to enable the Pharaoh's body to rise to the sky.

The building of the pyramids
We do not know exactly how the pyramids were built. Although some stone was quarried nearby, any granite used was brought by river from Aswan and white limestone casing for the pyramids was brought on boats from the eastern bank of the Nile. The stone was dragged on rollers from the edge of the river to the site of the pyramid. The ground which would form the base of the pyramid had to be leveled and then ramps were built so that the stones could be dragged up for each

section of the construction process. The core was built first and then the outer facing was put on, working from the top of the pyramid to the ground. The ramps were gradually removed as each section was completed.

The laborers and craftsmen used simple tools of bronze and stone. After many years' work the pyramid was ready. Once the coffin had been dragged into the burial chamber, the entrance was blocked and hidden. Most tombs were robbed and their stones were re-used for other buildings.

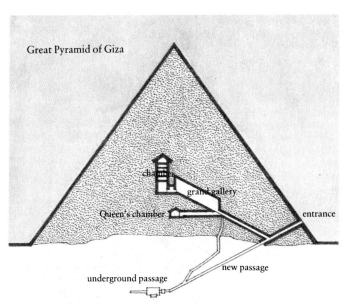

Great Pyramid of Giza

chamber

grand gallery

Queen's chamber

entrance

underground passage

new passage

Cross-section of the Great Pyramid at Giza. The plan was altered twice during construction. The pyramid was robbed, probably at the end of the Old Kingdom.

Building a pyramid.

Rock Tombs and Funerary Temples

Valley of the Kings

By the beginning of the New Kingdom most pyramids had been plundered. The Pharaohs of the 18th Dynasty chose to be buried less conspicuously, in tombs that were hidden away.

From the time of Tuthmosis I (c. 1520 BC), they were buried in rock-cut tombs in a remote valley on the west bank of Thebes, now known as the Valley of the Kings. Earlier Theban rulers were buried in tombs to the north of the Valley. 62 tombs have been discovered in the Valley.

In order to keep the position of the tombs secret, the funerary temples for the worship of the dead rulers were built far away, at the edge of the cultivated land.

The tombs were cut into the cliffs and consisted of a long corridor with several halls which ended in a burial chamber. They were decorated with religious scenes showing the Pharaoh in the presence of the gods and all the things he would see in the next world. There were also religious texts and spells to protect the Pharaoh against danger.

Only the tomb of the young king Tutankhamun has been found unplundered. Its contents give some idea of the immensely rich burials of these Pharaohs (page 84).

Mortuary temple of Queen Hatshepsut at Deir el-Bahri, the place traditionally associated with the goddess Hathor. Part of the temple is cut into the rock and part is freestanding.

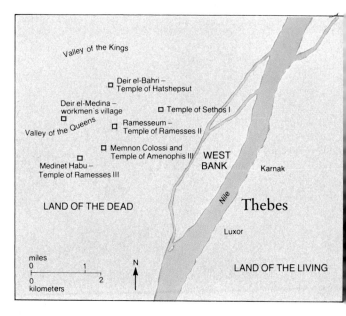

The earliest and main part of the town of Thebes and the principal temples were on the east bank. Across the river were the mortuary temples and royal and private tombs.

Valley of the Queens

From the time of Ramesses I, the Pharaoh's wives were buried separately. The tombs of the Queens and several princes who died in a smallpox epidemic in the reign of Ramesses III are in the Valley of the Queens. Some of the 70 tombs here were never finished, but those that were completed are delicately colored and very beautiful. The young princes are shown being introduced to the gods by Ramesses III.

Elsewhere, other members of royalty were also buried richly, and in a smaller valley the tomb of three princesses of the reign of Tuthmosis III contained vessels of gold and silver.

Non-royal tombs

Apart from the royal tombs, there are many private tombs including those of high officials, called the Tombs of the Nobles. Unlike the royal tombs, they are decorated with scenes of daily life as well as religious texts and scenes. Much has been learned about aspects of Egyptian life from these wall-paintings.

THE LAND OF THE DEAD

The tomb of the scribe and astronomer Nahkt, and that of an earlier scribe, Menna, have scenes of the harvest and of fishing and hunting. In the tomb of Rehkmire', he is shown being installed as vizier. There are also scenes of tribute bearers from foreign lands and another of temple workshops, together with funerary scenes and offerings to the gods Osiris and Anubis. The tomb of Sennefer, the vizier of Thebes under Amenophis II, is decorated with a vine laden with grapes, while that of Userhat, the scribe and tutor to this Pharaoh, has a scene showing barbers at work. There are many other private tombs dating from the 6th Dynasty to Greek and Roman times in the Theban City of the Dead.

Funerary temples

Also on this western bank are the remains of temples, which stretch for some 4 miles. Most of these were royal mortuary or funerary temples, where the cult of the dead kings, hidden in the rock-cut tombs, was carried out. But some date from the Graeco-Roman period.

Queen Hatshepsut built her beautiful mortuary temple at Deir el-Bahri. The temple, which is terraced, has three graceful colonnades. It was approached from the valley temple (now destroyed) along a massive causeway lined with sphinxes. Ramps led to the colonnades, with open courts on either side. There were trees and flower-beds and many statues. Incense trees were brought from Punt to be planted here and the Queen had the southern half of the middle colonnade decorated with scenes of the expedition to Punt.

At the mortuary temple of Ramesses II, known as the Ramesseum, stood huge statues of the Pharaoh, called colossi. The *pylons* of the temple are decorated with battle scenes. The temple of Ramesses III, Medinet Habu, was part of an enormous complex which was used later as an administrative center for the city of Thebes.

Howard Carter and Lord Carnarvon opened the tomb of Tutankhamun in November 1922. "Surely never before in the history of excavation has such an amazing sight been seen..."

The Boy King

Tutankhamun's tomb discovered

On 6 November 1922, the Egyptologist Howard Carter sent a telegram to the fifth Earl of Carnarvon. "At last have made wonderful discovery in valley; a magnificent tomb with seal intact; recovered same for your arrival; congratulations." The tomb that was subsequently opened, on 26 November, is now the most famous of all Egyptian tombs—that of the young king Tutankhamun, who had reigned during the 18th Dynasty.

Among the Egyptian records of royal tomb-robberies there was no mention of Tutankhamun's tomb having been plundered.

Carter had become convinced that this tomb was hidden somewhere in the Valley of the Kings and had never been found by tomb-robbers. Lord Carnarvon had developed a great interest in

Tutankhamun's gilt throne. The back is decorated with a scene showing the seated king and his wife Ankhesenpaten. Above them is the sun-disk with rays ending in life-giving hands.

Egyptology and had financed Carter's work for five years.

On 1 November Carter started to excavate near the tomb of Ramesses VI. Two days later a small boy found a step buried in the sand.

The steps led down to a walled-up doorway. Carter immediately sent his telegram to Lord Carnarvon, who arrived in Egypt on 23 November. The entrance was uncovered and at the end of the entrance passageway was a second doorway. Carter made a small hole and held up a candle. At first he could see nothing, but presently, "as my eyes grew accustomed to the light, details of the room within emerged slowly from the mist, strange animals, statues and gold—everywhere the glint of gold."

It is the only Egyptian tomb ever to be found virtually intact. In the first room were beds, chariots, ebony and ivory stools, chests, vases, and linen robes, all in disarray. The burial chamber contained a huge wooden shrine covered in gold. Beyond, lay a room with a gold shrine, chests, model boats, and a statue of Anubis.

It took several years of patient work before the whole tomb was emptied. The contents were removed and are now mostly in the Cairo Museum. The young king's body was re-buried in the tomb.

Egyptian treasures rediscovered

In 1987 the seventh Earl of Carnarvon was preparing an inventory of the contents of his ancestral home, Highclere Castle, with the help of a retired butler, Robert Taylor. His grandfather and Howard Carter had done much of their work at Highclere, but since then the Egyptian connection had been broken. Lord Carnarvon had known the house since his childhood, so when Robert Taylor showed him two hidden cupboards he had never seen before, he was amazed. Inside these cupboards the two men found hundreds of Egyptian objects from Carter's excavations, which had been completely lost for over 60 years. Nobody can be sure how the treasures come to be hidden for so long, but using Carter's notes and published reports, archaeologists can now identify the objects precisely.

Right: The seventh Earl of Carnarvon with a figure of Harpocrates, who is the god Horus represented as a child.

Another missing chapter in the story of Carnarvon and Carter was brought to light in May 1988 by Christian de Tutundjian, a student at the Institute of Archaeology, London. He discovered that some seeds he had been sent for his studies by the Wood Museum in Kew Gardens had never been properly entered in the Museum's catalogue. Instead, there was a sentence reading "samples believed to have been given by Carter in 1924". Where precisely had the seeds come from? Nobody had checked.

Hunting through store-rooms in Kew, Christian discovered more and more boxes full of seeds, each marked with a number. In one of the boxes there was part of what seemed to be a wreath of flowers. Could such a hoard of seeds perhaps be from the tomb of Tutankhamun? The only way to be sure was to compare the numbers on the boxes

Right: The seventh Earl of Carnarvon with a figure of Harpocrates, who is the god Horus represented as a child.

with a catalogue of Carter's finds. Christian knew that there was just such a catalogue in the Institute of Archaeology. He raced back to check—the numbers matched. The seeds and wreath were indeed some of those placed over 3,000 years before in the tomb of Tutankhamun, discovered by Carter, sent for analysis to Kew but then completely forgotten.

It is thought that there are more than 50 species of plants in each of the 30 boxes discovered. Now archaeologists and botanists are able to analyze them to form a clearer picture than ever before of farming and life in ancient Egypt.

Left: Portion of a wreath from Tutankhamun's burial, as it was rediscovered in a box sent to Kew Gardens, London, by Howard Carter. The wreath was made of olive leaves, cornflowers and other flowers.

Egypt Then and Now

The end of the Pharaohs

The death of Cleopatra symbolized the end of Egypt of the Pharaohs (known as Pharaonic Egypt). But in fact, that world of powerful god-kings had ended nearly a thousand years earlier.

Under the last Ramesside Pharaohs the country had become weak and eventually the two lands were divided. Egypt had come to depend more and more on foreign mercenary soldiers who then settled there. In the 10th century B.C. Libyans, who had settled in the Faiyum, established a dynasty of kings. Eventually only the outer forms of the ancient Egyptian civilization continued and foreigners contended for the throne—Nubians, Assyrians, and Persians in turn.

The great changes that took place within the country affected the "institutions." This is the term used by scholars to describe those powerful groups that establish and control the rules by which ordinary people live—in other words, the kingship, the law, religion, and the nobility.

Life remains unchanged

The lives of the majority of Egyptians continued unchanged in essentials throughout Pharaonic and Ptolemaic Egypt. Naturally, they were affected by natural disasters, such as excessive flooding or plagues. So too, economic problems and disorder in the land had their effect and resulted in suffering. Until the spread of Christianity during the Roman era, there was little fundamental change in the culture of the peasants.

For these people, changes in the seat of power and the coronation or death of kings were far less important than changes such as new techniques in irrigation, which directly affected their daily lives.

For example, in the 6th century B.C. the Persians introduced the *saquiah*, a wheel driven by oxen, connected with another wheel with earthenware pots which lifted water from one level and emptied it at a higher level. Later the *tambour* or Archimedes screw came into use. This lifted water over a short distance. Earlier, *shadufs* had been used to transfer water from one place to another and these are shown in wall-paintings of the 19th Dynasty. They can also still be seen on the banks of the Nile today.

The Aswan Dam

The greatest change for those working on the land has been the building of the Aswan Dam in 1968. This catches the water in Lake Nasser and means that the flow of the Nile is now controlled

Below left: Wall painting from an 18th Dynasty tomb showing mud bricks being made in a wooden mold. Straw was added to bind the mud together.
Below right: Even today bricks are still made in the ancient way.

mechanically. The annual flooding of the river therefore no longer takes place. The loss of the silt left behind after the flooding has meant that farmers must now use fertilizer. This has to be paid for, so the cost of producing food has increased.

There have also been unforeseen problems. The annual flooding used to flush out the ground and remove the salt. Now the ground is becoming salty, which means that plants do not grow so well. In time, this soil could be transformed into desert.

On the other hand, the dam has enabled electricity to be brought to the villages, which until recently looked almost identical to those from ancient times. Now the mud-brick houses, still constructed of bricks made in the ancient way, have electricity cables and television antennas.

In many remote villages it is still possible to think that you are not in the modern world. The peasants, called the *fellahin*, work the fields in their loincloths and many of the crops they tend have been grown from the earliest times. The date-palm is still an important source of food and drink.

Egyptian religion

Apart from electricity and tractors, the main visual difference between an ancient Egyptian village and a modern one is the presence of the mosque and, in some places, the Coptic Church. Egypt remained Christian until the arrival of the Arabs in A.D. 640. Since that time it has been an Islamic country, although some families remained

A mosque constructed within the walls of the Temple at Luxor.

Above left: 18th Dynasty wall-painting of a plowing scene.
Above right: A modern scene showing a man working his field using a plow which has hardly changed from the ancient style.

Christian. These Christians (called Copts, from the Greek word for Egypt) are the descendants of the ancient Egyptians. In their church services Coptic, the last form of the ancient language, is used.

Arabic is now the language of the Egyptians. The big cities, with their mosques and bazaars are not unlike those of many Arab countries.

Yet in the country and away from the towns, the river, trees, and sun persist and reflect the permanence of the landscape. In spite of modern electric pylons, the views of the palms, villages, sailing boats on the river, and the thin strip of green valley stretching below the cliffs are little different now from those of Ancient Egypt.

TIMELINE

Note: Scholars do not always agree on the dates of events in Egyptian history. The dates here have been rounded to the nearest century or decade.

B.C.	
5000–3100	**Neolithic** cultures in Upper and Lower Egypt, developing into **Pre-dynastic** settlements.
c. 3100	**Archaic Period**: first two dynasties; Union of Upper and Lower Egypt by Menes. Capital at Memphis. Brick tombs at Abydos and Saqqara; large-scale irrigation.
2680–2180	**The Old Kingdom**: Dynasties 3 to 6. Pyramid Age; step pyramid, Great Pyramid and Sphinx at Giza; mastaba tombs of nobles at Saqqara. Heliopolis center of sun-god Re'; trade with Byblos; wars with Libyans and Nubians; expeditions to Sinai; large-scale stone building and sculpture. Rise of feudal nobles and decline of royal authority. Kings: Djoser, Khufu, Khephren, Pepi II.
2180–2050	**First Intermediate Period**: Dynasties 7 to 10. Civil war; rival kings; breakup of united kingdom; hard times.
2050–1780	**The Middle Kingdom**: Dynasties 11 to 13. Egypt reunited by Mentuhotep II: Thebes the capital, beginning of rise of Amun. 12th Dynasty rule from Itjawy near Memphis. Nobles suppressed; Nubia conquered; Buhen fort built; increase in wealth.
1780–1560	**Second Intermediate Period**: Dynasties 14 to 17. Asiatic Hyksos control northern Egypt and Nubia is independent and in alliance with Hyksos. The south ruled by Theban princes.
1560–1085	**The New Kingdom**: Dynasties 18 to 20. 'Ahmose expels the Hyksos; Egypt becomes an imperial power.
1560–1300	**Dynasty 18**: Egypt's domains extend from Nubia to Euphrates. Hatshepsut sends expedition to Punt. Thebes the capital; Luxor and Karnak temples; Valley of the Kings; Amenhotep IV (Akhenaten) fails to establish Aten as sole god; Tutankhamun restores Amun; Horemheb destroys the city of Akhetaten.

B.C.	
1300–1200	**Dynasty 19**: Seti I and Ramesses II maintain empire; fight against the Hittites; temples built at Abydos, Abu Simbel and Karnak.
1200–1085	**Dynasty 20**: Ramesses III last of the great kings, repels Libyans and Sea People. Egypt's military power declines; provinces in Palestine and Syria lost; royal tombs looted; High-Priests of Thebes become powerful. Under last Ramesses, Egypt effectively divided; north ruled by Smendes, south by Herihor. Nubia lost.
1085–716	**The Third Intermediate Period**: Dynasties 21 to 24. Egypt now splintered into different domains; south controlled by family of High Priest of Amun; north by Libyan and other dynasties.
716–333	**The Late Period**: Dynasties 25 to 31. Nubian and Saite rulers. Peaceful.
c. 670	Assyrians sack Memphis and Thebes.
525	Persians conquer Egypt. Later expelled and Dynasty 30 are the last Egyptian rulers. Persians return.
332	Alexander the Great conquers Egypt.
304–30	**Ptolemaic Dynasty**.
37	Cleopatra VII marries Mark Antony.
30	Octavian (Augustus) defeats Cleopatra and Mark Antony. Egypt becomes a Roman province.

The Palermo Stone. A stone inscription providing details about kings and events until the third ruler of the 5th Dynasty. The King's name is in the first line; the second and third lines give the event and the height of the Nile. It is an important document for dating the early period of Egypt's history.

GLOSSARY

amulet small charm to ward off evil spirits; placed on mummy and worn as jewelry.

Book of the Dead prayers and instructions to help the dead person on his or her journey to the afterlife. Placed in tomb; written on papyrus.

Ba an aspect of the personality, the soul.

canopic jars four jars in which internal organs were placed to preserve them for the next world. Lids were animal shaped, symbols of four sons of the god Horus.

cartouche oval shape in which the king's name is written in hieroglyphs.

cataract places in the Nile where the river is full of rocks and boulders.

colossus an enormous statue of a god or king.

demotic everyday writing of the late period.

dynasty a family of kings succeeding each other. Egypt's history is divided into 31 dynasties.

embalming preservation of a dead body using oils and spices, after body had been dried.

hieratic flowing form of writing based on hieroglyphs; used by priests and scribes.

hieroglyph picture of an object standing for a word or sound; the first form of Egyptian writing.

Hyksos probably originally migrants from Palestine; ruled the north after Middle Kingdom.

hypostyle hall many-columned temple hall.

inundation annual Nile flood which covered the land in July–August. Receded September. Left layer of fertile silt for crops.

irrigation method of supplying land with water by means of channels leading from a central source.

Ka spirit of a person which lived on in death: offerings of food and drink for the ka placed in the tomb.

kohl eye-paint made either of crushed green malachite stones or ground carbon.

mastaba brick-built, rectangular "bench shaped" tomb; from Arabic word for bench.

Memphis capital of the Old Kingdom.

mummy a body from which internal organs were removed; it was then wrapped in bandages to preserve it.

natron sodium compound, yellow color, used for mummification.

nome Greek term for the districts into which Egypt was divided for administration purposes.

Nubia country lying to the south of Egypt.

obelisk tall pillar tapering to the top; gilded tip; originally connected with worship of sun god at Heliopolis, but later placed in front of temples.

ostracon (plural **ostraca**) a potsherd or piece of broken pottery; used for writing on.

palette used for mixing eye paints. In Pre-dynastic times large ceremonial palettes were carved with animals or scenes of important events.

papyrus a tall reed with a large head of feathery shape used for making paper, baskets, rope, sandals, light boats, and mats. The word is also used to describe both the writing material and the written document.

pectoral piece of jewelry, usually rectangular, worn round the neck; often made of gold.

pharaoh from the word for "Great House" ie. the royal palace. The word came to be applied to the king. The Egyptians regarded their king as a god.

Ptolemaic Period Alexander's general Ptolemy took control of Egypt after Alexander's death. Ptolemy's descendants ruled as Pharaohs. This period ended when the Romans defeated Cleopatra and Mark Antony.

Punt the location of the incense-producing region is not exactly certain; either the present-day Yemen or the horn of Africa's coast.

pylons great sloping walls of temples.

scarab a sacred beetle; used as an amulet.

scribe one who wrote; usually an official or priest; he kept records of public events and calculated tax yields, wages, etc.

shabti or **ushabti** a small magical statue buried with the dead peson to do his work for him in the afterlife.

shaduf a simple irrigation machine for lifting water; it consisted of a long pole attached to an upright post, at one end of which was a counter-weight, and at the other, a bucket.

Sinai country to the east of Egypt at the northern end of the Red Sea.

sistrum musical instrument made of metal and shaped like a rattle; made a jingling sound.

sphinx mythical beast with a man's head.

stela an upright slab or pillar usually with an inscription.

Thebes capital of the New Kingdom.

LOOKING FURTHER

If you now want to have a look at Egyptian *evidence*, you will find that there is plenty to see in many museums. So many objects have been collected over the years that even fairly small towns and some country houses have Egyptian collections. There are over 500 museums in the world with good Egyptian collections, so wherever you live you should be able to see objects like those in this book. Here are a few of the main museums to visit, depending on where you live. Some museums have talks and films about Egypt.

U.S.A.
Walters Art Gallery, Baltimore.
Museum of Fine Arts, Boston.
Oriental Institute Museum, Chicago.
Art Museum, Cincinnati.
Brooklyn Museum, New York.
Metropolitan Museum, New York.
Pennsylvania Museum, Philadelphia.
University Art Museum, Princeton, New Jersey.
Art Museum, Seattle.

United Kingdom
British Museum, London.
Petrie Collection, University College, London.
Victoria and Albert Museum, London.
Horniman Museum, London.
City Museum, Bristol.
Fitzwilliam Museum, Cambridge.
Gulbenkian Museum of Oriental Art, Durham.
Royal Scottish Museum, Edinburgh.
Art Gallery and Museum, Glasgow.
Merseyside County Museum, Liverpool.
University Museum, Manchester.
Ashmolean Museum, Oxford.

Europe
Staatliche Museen, Agyptisches Museum, E. Berlin.
Agyptisches Museum, W. Berlin.
Musées Royaux d'Art et d'Histoire, Brussels.
Nationalmuseet, Copenhagen.
National Museum of Ireland, Dublin.
Rijksmuseum van Oudheden, Leiden.
Staatliche Sammlung Agyptischer Kunst, Munich.
Louvre, Paris.
Musée du Petit Palais, Paris.
Museo Capitolino, Rome.
Museo Barracco, Rome.
Museo Gregoriano Egizio, Vatican, Rome.
Institut d'Egyptologie, Strasbourg.
Museo Egizio, Turin.

INDEX

Page numbers in *italics* refer to illustrations.

A
Abu-Simbel, temples at 18, *19*
Abydos 24
agriculture *see* farming
'Ahmose (Theban king) 36
Akhenaten 37, 42–3, *43*
Akhetaten (el-Amarna) 18, 41, 42, 43, 50, 52
Akkadian language 18, 41
Alexander the Great 20, 47–8, *49*
Alexandria 48
Amarna Age, The 42–3
Amenophis I 37
Amenophis III 36, *36*, 42
Amenophis IV 37, 42
amulets 61, 68, 75, 76
Amun (god) 30, *32*, 33, 37, 42, 43, 49
    temple of 34–5, *34*, *35*
animals 32, 54, 56, 66, *66*
antiquities 15, 16
Anubis (god) 76, 84
Arabic language 87
archaeology 16–18
Archimedes screw 86
army 38–9
Artemidorus *48*
Asia, contacts with 40–1, 46–7
Assurbanipal, King of Assyria 46
Assyria 40, 46, 86
Aswan 13, 50, 86–7
Aten (sun-god) 37, 42–3
Atum (sun-god) 32

B
ba-bird 74
Babylonia 18, 40, 41, *41*, 46
banquets 54, 58–9, *58*
bead-making 62
Beni Hasan *12*
Bes (god) 30, 51
birds 56, *57*
"Black Land, The" (Keme) 12

Book of the Dead 77
bow-drills 62
Buhen, fortress of *11*
burials, *see* funerals; mummies
Byblos 40

C
Cambyses, King of Persia 46
canopic jars 75
Carnarvon, Fifth Earl of *83*, 84
Carnarvon, Seventh Earl of 84, 85
carpentry 63, *64*
Carter, Howard *83*, 84–5
cartouches 20, *21*
cattle 66
causeways 34
Champollion, Jean François 20–1, *21*
chariots 37, 38, *39*
Christianity 14, 15, 49, 87
Cleopatra VII 49, 86
Cleopatra's Needle *11*
clothing *24*, *27*, 60–1, *60*
Colossi of Memnon *36*
copper 23
Copts 20, 87
corvée duty 28
cosmetics 60, *60*, 61
crafts 62–3, 64–5
Crete 40, *41*
crime 28
crowns, kings' *23*, *27*, 27
cult temples see under temples
Cyrus, King of Persia 46, 68

D
Dahshur, pyramid at 78, *78*
dancers *58*, 59
Darius, King of Persia 68
dates (date-palms) 55, 87
dates (historical) listed 88
Deir el-Bahri *15*, 74
    temple of Hatshepsut *11*, 40, 82, *83*
Deir el-Medinah 18, 50–1, *51*
della Valle, Pietro 14
Delta of Nile 13, 45, 56

demotic writing 20
Diodorus 67
Djoser, pyramid of 24, *25*, 26, 78, *78*
doctors 68–9
drawing techniques *63*
drink 54, *55*
dynasties 24–5, 88

E
education 72, *73*
Edwin Smith Papyrus 68
Egyptology 16
el-Amarna *see* Akhetaten
Esarhaddon, King of Assyria 46, *46*
evidence 14–21
excavations 16–17, *16*, *17*, *18*

F
faience 62
Faiyum, The 13, 25, 45
farming 22, 66–7, *66*, *67*, 87, *87*
    administration of 28
    under Ptolemies 48
    see also foods
fellahin (peasantry) 87
festivals 26, 27, 30, 58
fishing 56
flooding of Nile *see inundations*
foods 54–5, 56
    see also farming
fortresses *11*, 38
fowling 56
funerals 75, 76, 77, *77*
    see also mummies
furniture 52, *52*

G
games 58, *59*
Geb (god) 32, *32*, *33*
Giza, pyramids at *10*, 24, 78, *78*, 79
glossary 89
gods and goddesses 26, 32–4, 42–3, 48
    see also priests; temples; *and under names of individuals*

gold 13, 40
   goldsmiths 62, 65
granaries *50*
Greeks 48

H
Hapi (god) *32, 33*
Harkhuf, tomb of 24
Harpocrates (Horus) *85*
harvesting *67*
Hathor (goddess) *32, 33, 59, 82*
Hatshepsut, Queen II, 36, *82, 83*
heb-sed (Jubilee) 26, *26, 27, 78*
Heliopolis *11, 28*
herbs in medicine 69
Herodotus 12, 66, 75
Hierakonpolis 22, *23*
hieratic writing 20, *20*
hieroglyphics 20, *20–1, 21, 23,
   23*
High Dam (Aswan) 50, 86–7
Hittites 37, 41, *41, 43, 44*
honey 55, *55*
horses 41
Horus (god) 23, 27, 30, *32, 33,
   85*
houses 23, 50–3, *51, 53, 87*
hunting 54, *56, 57*
Hyksos people 25, 36, 38
hypostyle halls 34, *35, 35*

I
Imhotep 24, *25*
incense 40
industry 62–3, *64–5, 86*
inscriptions 24, *88*
instruments
   musical 58–9, *58, 59*
   surgical *69*
inundation (of Nile) 12, *13, 16,
   49, 50, 87*
   farming 22, 66
   Hapi 33
   Nilometers 28
Ipet-isut 34
irrigation 12, 22, 26, 28, 66, 86
Isis (goddess) 32, *32, 33*
Islam 87

J
jewelry 23, 61, *61, 62, 75*

K
ka (life-force) 74
Kamose (Theban king) 36
Karnak 34, *34, 35, 36, 42*
Kassite people 40
Khephren 24, *27*
Khnumhotep *24*
Khufu, Great Pyramid of *10*, 24,
   78, 78, 79
kings 88
   Amarna age 42–5
   foreign 46–7
   New Kingdom 36–7, 38
   Old/Middle Kingdoms 24–8,
     38
kohl 60, *61*
Kush 40

L
lapis lazuli 41, *61, 62*
leather-work 63, *64*
Libyans 44, 45, 86
literature 70–1
Luxor 35, *87*

M
Ma'at (goddess) 30, *32, 33*
maps *11*
   ancient 62
   foreign powers *41, 45, 47*
   Nile *13*
   Thebes *82*
Mark Antony 49
Maru-Aten palace 43
mastabas 24
medicine 68–9, *69*
Medinet Habu, Temple of 44,
   83
Megiddo, Battle of 38
Meidum *28*
Memphis 13, *16, 17, 25, 46*
Menes 23
Menna, tomb of *82*
Mentuhotep 24
Merneptah 44, *45*

metals, precious 62, *65*
Mitanni people 40, 41
mortuary temples see under
   temples
mummies *14, 15, 16*, 68, *68*, 69,
   74
   mummification 74–5, *75*
   see also funerals
music 58–9, *58*

N
Nahkt, tomb of 82
Napoleon I *14, 15*
Narmer 23, *23*
Nebuchadnezzar, King of
   Babylon 46
Neferneferuaten-tasherit *42*
Neferneferure *42*
Nefertiti 43, *43*
Nephthys (goddess) 32, *32*
Nile, River 10, 12–13, *12, 13,*
   22, 28, 86–7
   farming 28, 66
   gods 26, *32, 33*
Nofret (wife of Rahotep) *28*
nomes (districts) 22, 29, *29, 38*
Nubians *11, 13*
   Hyksos 25
   rulers of Egypt 46, 86
   soldiers 38, *39, 40*
Nut (goddess) 32, *32, 33*

O
obelisks 34, *34*
Octavian 49
"Opening the Dykes" 26
Opening of the Mouth 77, *77*
Osiris (god) 30, 32, *32, 33*
ostraca 51, *63, 72*

P
paintings *63*
palaces 27, 43
Palermo Stone, The *88*
papyrus 10, 72, 77
   evidence from papyri 16, 51,
     68, 77
   manufacture 69

pectoral 61, 76
Peleset people 44
Persepolis 47
Persia 46–7, *47*, 86
Petrie, Flinders *16*, 17
pharaoh, origin of word 27
pharaohs see under kings
Philae, temple of *18*
potsherds 72, *73*
pottery 17, *17*, 23, 52, 62
priests 30–1, *31*, 48, 68, 77
    of Amun 42, 43, 46
    see also gods and goddesses;
      temples
Ptah (god) *17*, 17, 32, 33
Ptolemy 48
Punt, land of 40
pylons 34, *34*, 35, *35*, 83
pyramids *10*, 24, *25*, 78–9, *78*,
    79, 80–1

Q
Qadesh 37

R
Rahotep, Prince *28*
Ramesses II *10*, 35, 37, *37*, 41,
    83
Ramesses III 37, 44, 45, 82, 83
Re' (sun-god) 32, 33, *33*
recipe 55
"Red Land, The" (*Dashre*) 12
regalia, kings' 27, *27*
Rehkmire', tomb of 82
Renenutet (goddess) 66
"Report of Wen-Amun, The" 71
rescue archaeology 18, *19*
rituals
    funerary 77, 78–9
    kingship 26
    medicine 68
    priests 30–1, *31*
Romans 49
Rosetta Stone 15, *21*, 48

S
Sais 46, 68
Saqqara 24, 78, *78*

saquiah (water-wheel) 86
Sarapis (god) 48
satraps 47
scarab beetle 76, *76*
schools 72, *73*
scribes 63, 70–1, *70*
Sea People, The 44, *44*
Sekhmet (goddess) 32, *33*, 68
senet (game) 52, 58, *59*
Sennacherib, King of Assyria 46
Sennefer, tomb of 83
sequence dating 17
Sequenenre' II (Theban king) 36
Sesostris II 50
Seth (god) 32, *32*, 33
Seti I *30*, 35, 37, *74*
settlement sites 18
shabti figures (in funerals) 76, 77
shadufs 86
Shu (god) *33*
Sinai 38, 40
Sinuhe 70–1
sistrum *33*, *59*
Smendes (vizier) 45
Snofru, pyramid of 78, *78*
soldiers 38–9, *38*
stone-working 62–3
strikes 45
sun temples 34, 43
surgery 69

T
Taharqa 46, *46*
tambour 86
Tanis 13, 45
taxation 28
Taylor, Robert 84
temples 14, 34, 48
    cult *16*, *17*, 34–5, 43
    mortuary *11*, 40, *44, 45*,
      78–9, *79*, 82, 83
    see also gods and goddesses;
      priests
Thebes 13, 46, 72, 82–3, *82*
    gods 33, 36
    rulers of 24
tombs *10*, 14, *14*, 15, 16, 18, 24,
    50

rock-tombs 82–3, *82*
tomb-workers 50–1
Tutankhamun 82, *83*, 84–5,
    84, 85
tools, farming 67
toys 58, *59*
trepanation (surgery) 69
Tutankhamun 37, 43
    tomb of 82, *83*, 84–5, *84, 85*
Tuthmosis II 36
Tuthmosis III *11*, 36, 38
Tutundjian, Christian de 84–5

U
Userhat, tomb of 83

V
Valle, Pietro della *14*
Valley of the Kings 13, 16, 34,
    51, 82
Valley of the Queens 82
village life 50–1
viziers 28

W
wall paintings *22*, 24, 37, *42,
    76, 86, 87*
    as evidence 18, 26, 61, 77
Wawat 40
weapons 38, *39*
weaving 50, 63
wildfowling 56
wine 54, *55*, 66–7
writing equipment *70*
written evidence 14, 18, 20,
    20–1, 21, 88